SIMPLE PAPERS

ON THE

CHURCH OF GOD.

By C. E. STUART.

REVISED EDITION.

WIPF & STOCK · Eugene, Oregon

Wipf and Stock Publishers
199 W 8th Ave, Suite 3
Eugene, OR 97401

Simple Papers on the Church of God, Revised Ed.
By Stuart, C. E.
Softcover ISBN-13: 978-1-7252-7550-8
Publication date 3/30/2020
Previously published by Loizeaux, 1905

CONTENTS.

---o---

CHAPTER
I. HID IN GOD.
II. ITS PRESENT RELATION TO GOD.
III. THE ASSEMBLY OF CHRIST.
IV. THE BODY OF CHRIST.
V. THE BRIDE OF CHRIST.
VI. ITS RELATION TO THE HOLY GHOST.
VII. OF WHOM COMPOSED.
VIII. THE UNITY OF THE SPIRIT.
IX. THE MINISTRY OF THE WORD.
X. PRAYER AND PRAYER MEETINGS.
XI. WORSHIP.
XII. THE INSTITUTION OF THE SUPPER.
XIII. PRACTICAL TEACHING IN CONNECTION WITH THE BREAKING OF BREAD.
XIV. DISCIPLINE.
XV. ITS FUTURE.

SIMPLE PAPERS ON
THE CHURCH OF GOD.

CHAPTER I.

HID IN GOD.

THERE is a word with which Greeks, Jews and Christians were well acquainted, though each attached to it a different meaning. That word, which in Greek is *ecclesia*, is rendered into English by *church*, or *assembly*.

The town-clerk of Ephesus made use of it when he attempted, and with success, to calm the excited crowd in the theatre of the city, which prided itself on being the temple-keeper of Artemis the Great. "If Demetrius," he said, "and the craftsmen which are with him, have a matter against any man, the law is open" (rather, the law courts are being held), "and there are deputies (or proconsuls): let them implead one another. But if ye inquire anything concerning other matters, it shall be determined in a lawful assembly (*ecclesia*)." (Acts xix. 38, 39).

Had a Jew been interrogated about the *ecclesia*, the thought that would have been uppermost in his mind would have been the congregation of the Lord, the privileged nation of Israel called out from the rest of the nations. Of this assembly Stephen made mention in his memorable speech before the Sanhedrin on the day of his martyrdom (Acts vii. 38). Into this assembly no

Ammonite or Moabite could enter, even to their tenth generation forever; and the children of an Edomite, though descendants of Abraham, could only form part of it in the third generation (Deut. xxiii. 3–8). It was a privileged company indeed; for it was Jehovah's assembly, and is styled "the congregation of the Lord." He had a right therefore to limit it nationally to Israel, and to determine under what circumstances, and at what time, any who were not of the race of Israel after the flesh, should be numbered amongst it.

But Scripture teaches us about another assembly, called "the assembly of the living God" (1 Tim. iii. 15), and which the Lord Jesus Christ has been graciously pleased to call His own (Matt. xvi. 18). It is with this that Christians are familiar, and of which they form part. It is of this, too, that they speak when the word *church* falls from their lips. Very frequently do we meet with *ecclesia* applied to the Christian assembly in the pages of the New Testament. All the apostolic writers but Jude and Mark refer to it. The Lord Jesus Christ spoke of it as something new, and not then even in existence. "I say unto thee, That thou art Peter, and upon this rock I will build My Church; and the gates of hell (or hades) shall not prevail against it" (Matt. xvi. 18). An assembly peculiar in its formation, and imperishable in its nature—such are the characteristics of it, as here set forth by the Lord; and as He is the first in the sacred volume who speaks of it, so is He the last. In Matthew He speaks of it viewed as a whole. In Revelation He uses the word in the plural, because He views the Church in its local aspect, each local company being called the assembly (Rev. xxii. 16).

There was a time, then, when the Church, in the sense

in which the Lord used the term, did not exist. The Jewish assembly had been on earth, and could point to its history of about fifteen centuries' duration, before the assembly to which Christians belong had been once mentioned or called into being. Yet all that time, and for a far longer period than that, the Church of which the Lord first spoke had a definite place in God's thoughts, and, moreover, had always formed part, and a very important part, of that wonderful plan which God is working out to the display of His own glory and that of His Son.

Of these facts we become cognizant through the writings of the apostle Paul, who alone of the sacred writers treats at length of the Church of God.

That the Church formed part of the wonderful plan of God we learn from the epistle to the Colossians, in which the apostle tells those saints that it was given to him, as the minister by whom the mystery was revealed, to fulfil (or complete) the word of God (Col. i. 25). Now by this he did not mean that no further revelations on the part of God, beyond those already vouchsafed to him, were to be made. Paul was not writing of what we call the canon of Scripture. That was not complete when he died; for John did not lay aside his pen, if indeed he had commenced to use it, till after the departure of the apostle to the Gentiles to be with Christ. Many things were revealed to John in Patmos for which we should search in vain in the epistles of Paul. In what sense, then, was it given to the latter to complete the word of God? He, the only apostle who had persecuted the Church of God, was the honored instrument selected to reveal the dispensation, or economy, of the mystery of the Christ. The mystery, when thus revealed, completed the range of subjects of which it has pleased God in His Word to treat. Creation, the fall of man, the atonement, and the kingdom, had been declared by other instruments. By Paul was made known the mystery—Christ the Head, and His people the members of His body, the two making up the mystic man called "the Christ" (1 Cor. xii. 12; Eph. iii. 4). Thenceforth God's counsels, as far as He has been pleased to disclose them, stood all revealed, and the word of God was completed.

Further, we are authorized in stating that the Church, which was not made known in other ages unto the sons of men as it has now been revealed to God's holy apostles and prophets by the Spirit, was nevertheless no afterthought of His; for from the beginning of the world it had been hid in God, who created all things (Eph. iii. 9). The One who had planned the whole work of creation, and by His divine power had carried out His purpose, had all along kept hidden in the recesses of His bosom that wonderful secret, so closely connected with His glory and His counsels about His Son. Of this Paul was singled out to be the first exponent.

It was a service given to him to enlighten all as to the Christian dispensation. To every Christian, therefore, should God's teaching about the Church be interesting. None can say that it does not concern them. But, further, angelic beings are instructed by the disclosure of this secret; for not only are all to be enlightened as to the dispensation of the mystery, but the manifold wisdom of God is now by the Church made known to the principalities and powers in the heavenlies (Eph. iii. 9, 10).

Formed, then, so late in the world's history as the Church was, is it destined, it may be asked, to possess a mere ephemeral existence? By no means. For the epistle, which tells us that the mystery had been hid in God from the beginning of the ages, states clearly that the Church will ever abide. "Unto God," writes the apostle, "be glory in the Church in Christ Jesus throughout all ages, world without end. Amen" (Eph. iii. 21). The first heaven and the first earth will pass away; national distinctions, it would seem, will cease; but the Church will throughout eternity exist as something marked and distinct from every one and every thing which does not form part of it.

The mystery, therefore, we learn, was hidden in God from the beginning of the world, but was not spoken of till the Lord Jesus announced that He would build His Assembly; yet we may well believe that it was ever present to the divine mind, though, as God has not stated that, we as creatures are not in a position dogmatically to affirm it. Remembering, however, in what terms it is described in the New Testament, we seem to have adequate grounds to conclude that it was so. For it is the Body of Christ, and will by and by be openly owned as His Bride. It is also the building which grows to a holy temple in the Lord.

Surely, then, when God acted in creative power, and brought man upon this scene, a creature so different from all the others which He created and made,* we may well believe that He had in His mind that Man of which our frame, as we learn, is a figure. Again, when He provided for Adam the helpmeet, formed her out of the man, and brought her to him, are we not to believe that other thoughts than those simply of providing the man with a wife were in the divine mind, even thoughts about that

---

* First created, to make or prepare afterwards for the abode of man.

Bride which His Son would die to possess, and would sanctify to present her to Himself for His own joy forever? Is not Adam "the figure of Him that was to come"? (Rom. v. 14.) And when Solomon's temple was erected, the pattern of which God had given to David (1 Chron. xxviii. 19), and Jehovah graciously and openly took possession of it by the cloud of glory which filled the house, we may well believe that He looked on to that temple which He would build, formed not of material stones, however large and costly, but of stones infinitely more precious to Him, even "living stones," as Peter says, believers on the Lord Jesus Christ.

But if any think that by such remarks we are traveling beyond the bounds of sober thought, and entering the realms of airy speculation, such must certainly acknowledge that there was a moment in the life of the Lord Jesus on earth when the beauty of His Church, His Bride, came within the scope of His vision. For in the house with His disciples He spoke that parable of the kingdom which tells of a merchantman who, seeking goodly pearls, was satisfied when he had found just one pearl of great price. None at that time could have understood of what He was speaking. Afterwards they must have discerned the purport of His teaching. The one pearl of great price, its value and its beauty acknowledged by the merchantman, left him nothing to desire but to possess it. At what a cost that was done!

What, then, His disciples could not have understood at the first, some in these days have had opened up to them, and when reading that parable know who is intended by the merchantman, how He gave up all He possessed to acquire the pearl, and of what that one pearl is a figure.

CHAPTER II.

ITS PRESENT RELATION TO GOD.

WHEN God had brought Israel through the Red Sea as a people redeemed by power, they celebrated His goodness in song, and declared their wish to prepare for Him a habitation (Exod. xv. 2). The thought they expressed as the desire of their heart was a new one, but a right one; for, their redemption having been accomplished, God could thus dwell, and, as we learn afterwards (Exod. xxv. 8), He *would* thus dwell amongst them. And those who shared in that redemption were privileged to provide the materials—a willing offering from grateful hearts made glad by the exercise of delivering power on their behalf.

In the wilderness God dwelt in the Tabernacle, in the land His abode was the House; both habitations erected after patterns expressly given to Moses and to David, and from materials offered by His people on the first occasion, and by David on the second. Of course, whatever they brought must have borne, in one way or another, the impress of the Creator's hand; for they could only bring of that with which their God had enriched them. Creation, both animate and inanimate, was laid under tribute to yield what was wanted for Jehovah's habitation. Things useful, things costly, things precious, things beautiful, were provided in profusion for the Tabernacle in the wilderness, and the willingness of the people to offer was only checked by the announcement that nothing more was required (Exod. xxxvi. 5–7).

The Tabernacle gave place to the Temple. God, who had dwelt in the former, dwelt in the latter, till the bright cloud of glory, the Shechinah, departed from the House, as seen in vision by Ezekiel (x.); loth to go, yet unable to stay because of the iniquities of the children of Israel. From that time to the present, God has never dwelt in His house at Jerusalem. It was His house when rebuilt; the Lord acknowledged it as such, and He graced it by His presence as God's house, His house, on the occasion of His triumphal entry into the doomed city and temple. By and by, as Ezekiel shows, the Lord Jehovah will return to it, never again to leave it, the place of His throne, and the place of the soles of His feet, where He will dwell in the midst of the children of Israel forever (Ezek. xliii. 7).

In Jerusalem, then, He does not now dwell. Their house was left to the Jews desolate; that was its condition when God ceased to inhabit it. To outward eyes it looked grand and imposing. In His eyes, whose house it was, it was even then desolate; and that condition cannot alter till the Jews shall see Him, and welcome His return, saying, "Blessed is He that cometh in the name of the Lord" (Matt. xxiii. 38, 39). Has God, then, now no habitation upon earth? A Jew would surely say that He has not. A Christian should answer that He has; a habitation, however, different in character and formed of materials unlike any that Israel, Solomon, or men, could provide. For redemption having been accomplished, redemption by the blood of God's Lamb, and the exaltation of the Lord Jesus to heaven having been effected, God has formed for Himself by the Holy Ghost a habitation upon earth. Of old, *men* built for God His dwelling-place; now *He* has built one for Himself—a building to which His people cannot by their offerings contribute, yet without whom it could never have been made. And as the Tabernacle and the Temple were severally composed of materials provided in their natural state by the Creator of the universe, so God's present habitation bears the marks of the Creator's handiwork; for in creative power in grace God has acted, and formed for Himself the stones, living stones (1 Peter ii. 5), those who are a *new* creation in Christ Jesus, even believers on His name; and this habitation of God has several names, each one, of course, appropriate and expressive. It is the *house* of God, the *temple* of God, and the *assembly* of the living God. Of all these terms, when speaking of it, does the apostle Paul make use. Let us look a little into them.

A *habitation* of God. This teaches us that God can still dwell upon earth, though the Tabernacle has been for ages non-existent, and the Temple at Jerusalem has been for centuries laid low.

What a delight it evidently was to God to dwell amongst His people! He gathered Israel around Himself in the wilderness in an order which He was pleased to appoint (Num. ii.), and issued an injunction for the exclusion from the camp of every leper, every one that had an issue, and whosoever was defiled by the dead, "that they defile not their camps, in the midst whereof I dwell" (Num. v. 3). Again, at the close of their wilderness life, God reminded them, when speaking of the land of their inheritance, upon which innocent blood was not to lie unavenged, that He, the Lord, dwelt among the children of Israel (Num. xxxv. 34). And as He told Moses, so He told Solomon, of His dwelling among His people. Whilst the house was building, God cheered the king with the promise that, if he was obedient, the Lord would dwell among the children of Israel and not forsake them (1 Kings vi. 12, 13). After it was built God reaffirmed it, when He appeared to Solomon the second time, twenty years after the king had commenced to lay the foundations of the house of the Lord (1 Kings ix. 1-3). It is true the continuance of His presence was conditional on the king's obedience; yet surely God did delight to dwell among His people, and to tell them of it. But not less by deed, as well as by word, did the Lord proclaim this. When Moses had finished the erection of the Tabernacle, the cloud covered the tent of the congregation, and the glory of the Lord filled the Tabernacle (Exod. xl. 34). Not a day elapsed, after His earthly dwelling-place was made ready for Him, before the Lord openly and formally took possession of His habitation, to which none had invited Him, but out of which He would not consent to remain. Again, when Solomon had dedicated the house at Jerusalem, the cloud, which had rested on the tent of the congregation at Sinai, appeared afresh on mount Moriah, and filled the house; and the glory, which had prevented Moses from entering the Tabernacle, prevented the priests from standing to minister; for the glory of the Lord had filled the house of the Lord (1 Kings viii. 11). If God took a delight in dwelling in the midst of His people then, not less does He surely now, since He has made them His habitation in the Spirit.

The ideas, then, of God's habitation, God's house, God's temple, God's assembly too, are not new. Israel, in a way, could speak of them all as terms with which they were familiar, and could have turned to the written word for divine authority as to the use of them. But what was new, and is peculiar to Christian teaching, is the application of the terms "habitation," "house," and "temple," to *the company of God's people upon earth.* God is present upon earth, though His Son has been cast out of the world. He dwells too upon earth. He possesses, He acknowledges, a habitation peculiarly, really His own. "In Christ Jesus," writes Paul, "ye also are builded together for a habitation of God in the Spirit" (Eph. ii. 22). To this same building Peter refers (1 Pet. ii. 5). The apostle of the circumcision thus bears testimony to it in common with the apostle of the Gentiles, the one and the other reminding those specially under their charge of the privilege which was theirs. Those who had been formerly Gentiles, and therefore could never have entered within the inclosure of the Temple set apart for the race of Israel—those, too, who had been Jews, but had turned their backs on mount Zion as well as on mount Moriah, when they went forth to Christ without the camp—those both learnt how richly God had dealt with them in grace, in making them part of that which He deigns to call His habitation. Such was a privilege of those formerly Gentiles, far surpassing anything which they could have enjoyed as proselytes at Jerusalem. This, too, was the privilege of the believing remnant of the Jews, to which their fellow-countrymen, unless converted before the rapture of the saints, must ever remain strangers. It is, it must be, a privilege of a very high order to form part of the habitation of God upon earth by the Spirit.

This habitation, however, is also called God's *house.* Now, though to some the distinction between habitation and house may seem a trivial one, it is none the less real. A house is a habitation, but a habitation need not be a house. And though the habitation of God is said to be built, and the assembly at Corinth is called God's building (οἰκοδομή), it is nevertheless true that where Scripture uses the term house (οἶκος) with reference to the assembly of God, the context suggests distinctive teaching in connection with it. God's habitation is treated of by the apostle Paul when dwelling on the privileges of those who formed part of it. Of God's house he writes when reminding his readers of their responsibility in connection with it. Thus, addressing the Hebrews, he says to them, "Whose house" (God's house) "are we, if we hold fast the confidence and the rejoicing of the hope firm unto the end" (Heb. iii. 6). They would prove by steadfastness that they really were part of God's house. So Peter, reminding his readers that judgment must begin at the house of God (1 Peter iv. 17), adds, "And if it first begin at us," etc.

Again, addressing Timothy, Paul writes to his child in the faith to tell him how to behave himself in "God's house, which is the assembly of the living God" (1 Tim. iii. 15). The rules, the regulations, for a house are laid down by the master, the owner of it. And since the assembly is *God's* house, not man's, Timothy was to learn how to conduct himself in it. Every one would reckon it a monstrous intrusion for another person to set about the regulating of a house unless distinctly authorized by the master to do it. Men would naturally resent such an action on the part of their fellows, and no plea on the ground of taste or judgment would avail against their condemnation for arrogating to themselves a position and authority in a house which did not belong to them. The master, the owner, all would agree, and not a stranger, nor even an inmate, is the fitting person to say how his house is to be conducted. Shall men, then, be allowed their right in such a matter, and God be denied His? Now has not this been practically the case in Christendom? Christians, and in some cases those not even converted, have taken upon themselves, with the sanction of the community at large, to make rules and regulations for a house of which, if converted, they certainly form part, but which belongs to another, even to God. And such practices are openly justified, and commended as fitting and proper. Once, however, let the force of the term "God's house" sink into the heart, and the impropriety, as well as incongruity, of men drawing up rules for the guidance of that house will be fully apparent. Timothy even, apostolic delegate as he was (holding thereby a position which, Titus excepted, no one else that we know of was ever called to occupy), could not make any rules himself, but received them from the apostle. Timothy surely never dreamt, and the apostle never countenanced the idea, of any man or company of men laying down rules formed in their wisdom for the orderly government of God's house. Should not the very term "God's house" suggest to each one the propriety of learning from the Word what are God's rules for its guidance and government?

But this house is also called God's *temple*, the shrine, as it were, of the Deity who dwells in it. Twice in the New Testament do we meet with this designation, and both times it is used by the apostle Paul when writing to the same company of Christians, those gathered unto the name of the Lord Jesus Christ at Corinth. The context helps us here, also, to determine the import of the term, and the reason of its selection. In the first epistle (iii. 16), when warning teachers to beware of what they were teaching, he writes to the whole assembly there gathered: "Know ye not that ye are God's temple, and that the Spirit of God dwelleth in you? If any man defile the temple of God, him shall God destroy; for the temple of God is holy, such (οἵτινες, not which) ye are." With the consciousness that the assembly was God's temple, could they be indifferent to the introduction of false doctrine? Should any, too, remembering this character of the assembly, be careless as to the doctrines they taught? The temple would remind all of the holy character of the assembly, and therefore of the holiness which befitted it. Again, when speaking of the general company of God's saints on earth, and not of the local assembly merely at Corinth, the same apostle reminds them that Christians should be separate from evil, and from communion with unbelievers, on the ground that believers in the aggregate are the living God's temple, who will dwell in them, and walk in them (2 Cor. vi. 16). One sees at a glance that there is a force and a fitness in the term "temple" used in this connection of thought, which no other word could so well set forth. Gentiles as well as Jews knew what the word temple would imply.

Here another thing should be pointed out. When the apostle writes of God's habitation, or of God's house, he knows of but one such upon earth. Where, then, can it be found? For it is no ideal thing, no phantom, since Timothy was to know how to behave himself in it. But where is it? Jerusalem cannot produce it; St. Peter's at Rome cannot lay claim to be it. No cathedral, no building of wood, brick, iron or stone, is entitled to this appellation. God does not dwell in any such at present. He dwells in His own habitation which in Christ Jesus He has made for Himself by the Spirit. Understanding this, we have to correct our thoughts, and to change perhaps our language, which is the index to our thoughts; for we cannot go now to God's house as those of old did, and as saints will by and by (Psa. cxxii.). We indeed who believe form part of it. If, then, we talk of going to God's house when we mean that we are about to assemble ourselves with God's saints for worship or for prayer, do we not by our language show that we have lost the right thought of what His house really is? We are attaching to a building, or a locality, a term which now belongs only to a peculiar company of people upon earth. Distinctive Christian teaching is virtually set aside, or ignored, as long as such language is accepted as correct. It was correct language for a Jew. It will be correct language for all who worship Jehovah by and by (Micah iv. 2). But scriptural language is not of necessity Christian language, though Christian language—understanding by that what the Bible authorizes—must ever be scriptural, if real.

As regards the terms "temple" and "assembly," the usage of Scripture is different. They are applied to the local gathering as well as to the general company of Christians upon earth. (See 1 Cor. iii. 16; 2 Cor. vi. 16, for the application of the term temple; and 1 Cor. i. 1, 2; Acts xx. 28, for the use of the term church, or assembly.) Nor are these the only senses in which these words are used; for both the one and the other are employed when the true Church universal is the subject in hand (Eph. i. 22; ii. 21).

To a consideration of the word *assembly* let us now turn.

By God's assembly on earth is to be understood that company of people which, professedly at least, has been gathered out from the rest of mankind unto Him. At first it was, as in glory it will really be, composed only of true Christians; for such alone at first professed to be believers on the Lord Jesus Christ. After a time the assembly of God included others besides real believers, though none who did not profess to be Christians. Now, wherever the truth has spread, members of the assembly are to be found. And in every place where a few souls own the Lord Jesus Christ, there an assembly is regarded as existing. It may be like that in Laodicea, in which mere profession was the prevailing characteristic. It may be like that in Philadelphia, where faithfulness to Christ was a marked feature of it. But whatever may be the spiritual condition of the company locally gathered, if professedly called out to God, it is regarded in the Word as God's assembly in that locality, and has responsibilities of no mean order in consequence. How little is this understood by those who only outwardly bear the name of Christ! Profession, of course, should be true; but profession of itself entails responsibility; and all who bear the name of Christ by profession declare that they are members of the assembly of God.

Dismissing at present from our consideration of the subject the Assembly as it will be perfect in glory, in which none but real Christians will be found, let us confine our attention to the Assembly, in its different aspects, as viewed upon the earth at any one time. If *those who composed it* were before the apostle's mind, he could write of the assembly of the Thessalonians (1 Thess. i. 1). If the *country* in which such gatherings were, was to be expressed, he makes mention of the assemblies of Galatia, or of Asia (1 Cor. xvi. 1, 19). If he was thinking of the *localities* in which different companies met, he writes of the church, or assembly, in the house of Nymphas (Col. iv. 15), of Philemon (Phil. 2), or of Aquila (Rom. xvi. 5.). When he thought of the *spiritual character* of the members, he writes of the assemblies of the saints (1 Cor. xiv. 33). Viewing the churches in *relation to Christ*, Paul describes them as assemblies of Christ (Rom. xvi. 16). In relation *to God*, he styles it the assembly of God. And if its relation to the *Father* is uppermost in his mind, he can write of it as in God the Father (1 Thess. i. 1; 2 Thess. i. 1).

The Assembly of God! What a thought it gives us! God connecting Himself with a company of people on earth who had need of the atoning work of the Lord Jesus Christ, and confessed it.

And now we would ask, How does this term "Assembly of God" strike on the ear, or impress the mind of those who hear or read about it? There was one once who evidently felt in no light way its force. Paul has left on record, in the first epistle to the Corinthians, what it was to him; for, writing of his grievous sin before his conversion, he states that he persecuted the Assembly of God. Saints they were. Believers on the Lord Jesus such had proved themselves to be. Yet he does not term them saints or believers, but writes of the Assembly of God, thereby exposing his former undisguised and unmitigated hostility to the company gathered unto God (1 Cor. xv. 9). Could he have expressed in a stronger way what he did in mistaken zeal for God? How far wrong must he have been when he was a persecutor of the Assembly of the living God! Again, writing to the Corinthians to expose the grossness of their conduct at the Lord's Supper, he pertinently asks them, Would they despise the Assembly of God? (1 Cor. xi. 22). An answer to such a question should surely be prompt and unhesitating. Could any one who served God despise His Assembly? To a question so pointed, so searching, surely but one answer could be given. How the need there was for such a question shows of what our wretched hearts are capable.

In conclusion, habitation of God tells us of our privilege; house of God reminds us of responsibilities; temple of God warns us of its holy character; Assembly of God proclaims to whom it has been, professedly, at least, gathered out.

CHAPTER III.

THE ASSEMBLY OF CHRIST.

TILL Adam was formed we have no mention of Eve Till the Second Man appeared we have no doctrinal teaching about the Church. God brought Eve to Adam. Christ came to get His bride. When all was in paradisaical order upon earth, Eve appeared upon the scene. Into a world which knew not God, the Son of God entered; and upon this globe, on which Adam and Eve first met, did Christ die to possess the object of His choice. Adam had nothing to do but to welcome his helpmeet—God's best gift to that creature whom He had placed as head over this creation. Christ had everything to do to get His bride, and to fashion her according to the requirements of His heart. Only through death could He possess her. Yet to die was not enough. Service, personal and continuous, was and is still needful before presenting "the Assembly to Himself glorious, not having spot, or wrinkle, or any such thing; but that it should be holy and without blemish" (Eph. v. 27). A state of perfection this is to which fallen man could never attain, yet short of which the Second Man will not rest satisfied.

What interest, then, must Christ take in the Church! What a place must it occupy in His affections, when, to acquire it for Himself, He would die! and to have it holy and without blemish, He would charge Himself with constant service on its behalf! And if such is His purpose, and such His service to fulfil it, none surely of those who form part of the Assembly should think it a matter of small moment whether they know anything of the Church of God or not. Any willingly remaining in ignorance of Scripture teaching about it either manifest selfishness in only wishing to be assured of their own salvation, or indifference to the grace bestowed upon us in being allowed to share God's thoughts respecting it, and to understand in some measure Christ's interest in it.

What, then, are the Church's relations to Christ? It is His Assembly, His body, His bride. Something about each of these, as was natural, we learn from His own lips.

Of His Assembly, as such, He alone speaks. Local assemblies, indeed, are characterized by the apostle Paul as belonging to Christ (Rom. xvi. 16). This is true of all of them. Further, the same apostle describes the assemblies which were in Judea as in Christ (Gal. i. 22). This, too, was common to all of them; but it marked out the assemblies in Judea as distinct from any synagogue of the Jews. They were assemblies of Christ, and in Christ. Terms and truths these are of which no Jew could ever have made use, or have professed even to acknowledge. Christ, however, alone treats of the whole assembly as His.

Here it may be well to state that the Church is distinct from the Kingdom. All who form part of the Assembly are in the Kingdom; but all in the Kingdom do not form part of the Assembly. Every saint who will have left the earth ere the Lord returns to it shall reign with Christ (Rev. xx. 4); but every one of such will not be a member of His body, the Church. Saints before the cross were not members of His body; saints who will be on earth after the rapture of 1 Thess. iv. 15–17 will likewise never become part of that wonderful company. Kingdom truth is common to both the Old and New Testaments. It pervades the volume of revelation. Church truth is only taught us in the latter. In conformity with this, it is only subsequent to the introduction of the King upon the scene, and when the character of the Kingdom, during the time of His rejection by the Jews and the world, has been sketched out by Himself in parabolic teaching (Matt. xiii.), that we have any mention of His assembly (Matt. xvi.). Just as Eve was the latest production of the Creator's handiwork, so the Assembly, the body, the bride of Christ, is the last new subject of which the volume of inspiration treats. Eve, however, appeared when Adam's authority was owned, and his place in this creation unquestioned. The Church is only revealed when the Lord has been openly rejected, and the Cross, as the witness and expression of it, has to form a necessary part of His teaching.

Again, the introduction of the Church in its relation to Christ as His body and His bride necessarily reminds us of His manhood; for it is as man that He has both. Now His manhood is dwelt on in the Old as well as in the New Testament. But, since the Assembly is only gathered out whilst Israel has her bill of divorcement, and will be taken away ere Jehovah will comfort Jerusalem with the assurance that He is still her husband (the whole Church epoch being, as it were, a parenthesis in the prophetic stream of time), one understands why the Church, which has to do with the Lord as man, is nevertheless, though found in the gospel history, not met with in the writings of the Old Testament prophets. They wrote of the sufferings of Christ, and of the glories which should follow (1 Peter i. 11). Now the sufferings and glories of Christ concern all God's saints most intimately, and are closely connected with Kingdom truth. Hence the earthly people require to be informed of them. But the Church is essentially a heavenly thing; so Church truth is distinct from Kingdom truth, and fitly finds its place in that volume of inspiration which deals with the work of God amongst men during the rejection by Israel of their King.

Further, since the Church is only gathered out from the nations of the earth during the rejection of Christ by the Jews, for Scripture regards it as distinct from the Jews and the Gentiles (1 Cor. x. 32), we may see likewise the fitness of its mention in Matthew's Gospel, and of its absence from the histories of the other three Evangelists. For since it is as man that the Son of God stands in peculiar personal relation to the Church, it is plain that in the Gospel of John, which sets Him forth as Jehovah, such a subject would not be in place. In Luke too, who is occupied with the Kingdom and God's grace to man, the Lord Jesus is presented as the Son of man, a character which shows that He has to do with earth and man in the widest sense. One may understand, then, that the Church, which, though formed of believers from any and every nation to whom the word of grace has reached, yet is an election out of Jews and Gentiles, would not form part of the Holy Ghost's line of teaching, as given us by the beloved physician. In Mark's account, too, who narrates events very much in historical order, and has presented the Lord in servant character, as Prophet, or Teacher, who is at the same time the Son of God, dispensational teaching is not the character of his Gospel; so instruction about the Church lies beyond the limits within which that writer was to confine himself. It is the personal ministry of Christ in the gospel amongst men that he so graphically presents to his readers.

But in Matthew the Lord is presented as Immanuel, King of the Jews, though rejected by the people. To him, then, was it given to hand down the teaching of the Lord about the Kingdom during the King's absence from the earth. In accordance with this, the character of the Kingdom during His absence from the earth is dwelt upon at some length in those parables which are similitudes of the Kingdom of the Heavens; whereas in Luke the blessings to be enjoyed in the Kingdom form a prominent part of his teaching about it. Now since that was the line specially appointed for Matthew to take up, it is not difficult to see that the instruction which he was commissioned to communicate would not be complete without some notice of the Church. By the one who describes the active service of Christ in the gospel, not a word is said about the Church. By him who was empowered to relate what would be seen on earth in consequence of the Lord's rejection, the Church is specially mentioned. So what John must have heard in common with Matthew, and what Peter must ever have treasured up in his remembrance, finds no place in the Gospel of the son of Zebedee, nor in that of Mark either, in which, if written, as tradition tells us, after intercourse with Peter, one might naturally have looked for a special mention of it. To the son of Alphæus alone are we indebted, under God, for our knowledge both of the Lord's remarks about it, and of that service especially entrusted to Peter, the carrying out of which has been recorded by Luke in the Acts.

What a moment it must have been when that secret,

hitherto kept concealed, was first touched upon by the Lord! The period of His ministry, the district in the land, as well as the occupation of the Lord at the time, all are noted. After His rejection had been made manifest, and a short time before that brief glimpse of His millennial glory which Peter, James and John were permitted to witness, and when engaged in prayer, as Luke only has told us (ix. 18), with the twelve around Him, the Lord Jesus questioned them as to men's thoughts about Him. Men's thoughts were various, all wide of the mark, but all agreeing in this, that they did not discern in Him anything more than what they and their fathers had witnessed. John the Baptist, Jeremiah, Elijah, or as one of the prophets—such were the surmises of men, and with them the twelve were well acquainted. To the Lord's first question, then, there was a general response. To His second, "Whom say ye that I am?" addressed though it was to the twelve, one only replied. Peter answered, "Thou art the Christ, the Son of the living God." A prophet the Lord truly was, though different in character and person from all who preceded Him. Had Peter more discernment than the rest, that he only answered? He was indebted, we learn, to revelation from the Father for his knowledge of the person of the Lord Jesus Christ. Blessed was he to have received it; yet it was no glory to him that he knew it. Upon that, as Matthew states, the Lord proceeded to tell him that He would build His Assembly; for the rock on which it is built is the truth, as Peter confessed it, that He is the Christ, the Son of the living God.

Two things have we here about the Church of all importance to notice. The one, that Christ would build His Assembly. As yet, then, it had not existed. So none of the Old Testament saints, up to and including John the Baptist, formed part of it; for they had died before it began to be built. The other is, that the rock on which it is built is the truth of Christ's person, as revealed by the Father to Peter. Can, then, those who receive not that testimony form part of the Assembly which is built upon it? How should they be reckoned as part of that building, the foundation of which they repudiate? Take away the foundation, and the·Church has nothing to rest upon. Refuse to own that foundation, and such a one has no part or lot in the matter. What is built upon that rock death can never overcome. Against the Son of the living God who shall, who can, prevail? He died. Yes; but He rose—the witness that He could not be holden of death. Something enduring, something which death could not overthrow, something which no creature power should remove, the Lord was about to build, and that something was the Church.

The foundation of the Assembly thus declared, the rearing of it is written of and described elsewhere. Peter, a stone in the building—for the Lord distinctly shows that he was not the rock itself ("thou art Peter ($πέτρος$, *i.e.*, a stone), and upon this rock ($πέτρα$) I will build My Church," are His words)—makes clear to us who are the living stones (1 Peter ii. 5); and Paul acquaints us with the ultimate destination of that which is thus built (Eph. ii. 21).

Remembering the historical associations of the neighborhood in which the Lord Jesus was at that moment, not far certainly from the site of the city of Dan, the announcement of the stability of His Church has marked significance. Dan had been memorable for the attempt of Jeroboam, and that successfully, to turn the eyes of

Israel from Jerusalem and Jehovah, who dwelt therein, to the golden calves which he erected in Bethel and in Dan, that most northern city of his kingdom. The idolatrous worship there established has passed away; the calves, the altars, the priests—all in connection with it— have come to naught. What Christ would build, bound to no place upon earth, though existing amongst men, was never to pass away. Against it the gates of Hades should never prevail; for with it He connected Himself, and on the confession of His person as the Christ, the Son of the living God, this new, this everlasting building was to rest.

"My Assembly," He calls it, though not then built. True there were some of its stones in existence and surrounding the Builder at that very moment; pillars, too, some of them were, as they are called in Gal. ii. 9; but as yet not a stone had been laid in its place; the structure had not even been commenced. "I will build" most pointedly shows that. And that He builds that Assembly, which is elsewhere called the Church of God, on the *rock*—the truth as to His person—is a plain proof that none but those who confess Him can form part of God's Assembly as viewed in its universal character (Eph. i. 22, 23). But further: since Christ is the Builder, and the Assembly is His, what He builds must be solid, real, and substantial. That must ever abide. Imperfection can have no place there. So in this, the first mention of the Assembly, it is brought before us as the company who are really what they profess, Christians, not in name only, but in truth. No hay, no wood, no stubble, can find a place there. Stones, living stones only, are the materials with which Christ builds; for it is the Church, according to God's purpose, of which He here treats. Imperishable is the structure, firm the foundation, for it rests on the truth about His person, that He is the Christ, the Son of the living God.

With this Assembly He connects Himself. He calls it His. All that it would appear to outward eyes He well knew. Its great failings—which men, the world, would afterwards chronicle—were before His mind. Its failure in corporate testimony before the world was all present to His vision; yet He calls it His Assembly. His Name was to be indissolubly connected with it. How precious, then, must it be to Him! How gracious that He is not ashamed to call it His when it has caused reproach on His name!

From Himself, too, we learn something of the provision made for it. First, that evil within it may be dealt with; and, secondly, that His presence may be counted upon. Of both of these the Lord teaches us in Matt. xviii. 18-20.

As the Assembly is composed of those who had once been children of wrath, and in whom the flesh, sin, would yet remain, Christ well knew both how saints might fall, and the watchfulness of the enemy in order to introduce corruption into that which he cannot destroy. The Acts of the Apostles illustrates this in the history of Ananias and Sapphira. The Epistles of Paul, of John, and of Jude, attest it likewise. Christ therefore has invested the Assembly with authority to deal with offenders in its midst in the most solemn way: "Whatsoever ye shall bind on earth shall be bound in heaven; and whatsoever ye shall loose on earth shall be loosed in heaven." What an authority is this! Action taken upon earth—if rightly taken, of course—is ratified in heaven. God owns, and will firmly maintain, the judicial dealings of the Assembly. If it binds on a person his sin, it is bound in heaven. If it looses a person from his sins, by receiving the individual amongst them as one fit to be at the Lord's table, that act is confirmed in heaven. At Corinth that power was exercised, and the offending brother felt it. To the world it might seem a small matter that the individual was put away from the midst of God's saints for grievous sin. Yet, since in heaven the sentence was ratified, what Christian could afford to despise it? No miraculous power, it is true, accompanied that sentence, to strike terror into the heart of the Corinthian community at large; no vengeance from heaven visibly overtook the offender. The power that was wielded was nevertheless very great, and the brother dealt with sorely felt it (2 Cor. ii. 7). With what authority, then, is the Assembly invested! That man upon earth should give heed to admonitions from heaven, all would admit; but that the action of the Assembly on earth, whether in binding or loosing, should be ratified on high, was something new indeed. To the world, Church censure may seem a most impotent act. If done, however, under the guidance of the Holy Ghost, it is really most potent; for no creature power can annul it.

But not only has Christ declared that the Assembly is invested with such solemn, such weighty authority, He has also openly assured His people of His presence, even if it be reduced to the greatest possible weakness as regards numbers. Observe with what solemnity this is also introduced: "Again I say unto you" (or, if the reading of the Vatican and many other uncials be adopted, "Again, verily I say unto you"), "that if two of you shall agree on earth as touching anything that they shall ask, it shall be done for them of My Father which is in heaven. For where two or three are gathered together in My name, there am I in the midst of them." So divided, so rent by factions, the assembly might be, that only two or three would be gathered unto His name; but if so gathered, He would be in their midst. Again, the whole Christian community in a place might only number two or three. From that number, insignificant though it might appear, Christ would not be absent. The sole condition for His presence is, "Gathered unto (εἰς) My name." And when in the attitude of dependence, that is, in prayer—for it is of those met for prayer that the Lord speaks in verse 19—He promised to be in their midst; and if agreeing on that which they asked, His Father would grant their request. With what authority, again we would say it, is the Assembly invested! In what weakness, too, may it be found; but what a privilege may it enjoy—the presence of Christ in its midst!

At first believers were of one heart and one soul (Acts iv. 32). That did not continue. Ere the apostles had left the earth, division had manifested itself amongst the saints. Paul felt this (2 Tim. i. 15); John experienced it (3 John ix.); and we in our day witness it, and feel it. Believers are divided; the Assembly is split up into many sects and denominations. What, then, are we to do? To meet all as one body seems at present impossible. Shall we acknowledge the evil, and acquiesce in it? Shall we fold our hands, and sit down appalled at the magnitude and hopelessness of the task of getting all to see eye to eye? Christ has set before us a different work, viz., to learn what it is to be gathered unto His name, and to act upon it. Then we know what we could not before—the joy and the blessing of His presence in our midst.

Centuries have rolled by since that promise was given; yet it still holds good. And saints there are in these days who have found it to be still true. How little, however, it is understood! How little is the presence of Christ amongst His people really known! The condition necessary for its enjoyment He has clearly stated—gathered unto His Name. He is faithful who has promised; for He cannot deny Himself. Why, then, should any Christian remain a stranger to the conscious fulfilment of such a promise?

CHAPTER IV.

THE BODY OF CHRIST.

IN the closest of earthly associations, connected, too, by the nearest and dearest of ties known to man, does the Church stand in relation to Christ. It is His body. Nothing can be closer than that. It is His bride, with the assured prospect of being manifested as the Lamb's wife. Nothing can be dearer and nearer than that.

And first, as to His body, God has given "Him to be head over all things to the Assembly, which is His body, the fulness of Him that filleth all in all" (Eph. i. 22, 23). Of assemblies, God acknowledges but one, called here *the* Assembly, the same which is elsewhere termed the Assembly of the living God (1 Tim. iii. 15), and is claimed by the Lord Jesus Christ, as we have seen, as His own (Matt. xvi. 18). But this Assembly is also the body of Christ, which, viewed in this character, has Him for its head.

Now the headship of Christ is by no means an unimportant subject in the Scriptures, nor is it one in which but few have any concern. Far and wide throughout the universe does the headship of Christ extend. Further than the eye of man has yet penetrated is that headship to be acknowledged; for to three distinct spheres does the headship of Christ appertain. He is the head of all principality and power, as we learn from Col. ii. 10. Headship in this character has of course to do with His place in creation; and the mystery of God's will, now disclosed to us in Eph. i. 10, but not yet carried out, has made known the divine purpose of heading up all things in the Christ. Again, as the Christ, He is the head of every man, the man being, in his turn, woman's head (1 Cor. xi. 3). There is, however, a third character of headship in which the Lord is presented. "He is the head of the body, the Church: who is the beginning, the first-born from among the dead; that in all things He might have the pre-eminence" (Col. i. 18). The headship over the universe is His who died, and He receives it who created all things, being the first-born of all creation, and that by virtue of having called it all into being (Col. i. 15). His headship over every male as distinct from the female flows from His incarnation, who as man is the Christ. His headship in relation to the Assembly only dates from His resurrection; for until He had died the Assembly had no existence; but since He has died and has risen, He stands as head in relation to it. He is head of the body, the Church (Eph. i. 22; iv. 15; Col. i. 18; ii. 19); He is also head of the Church, as the husband is head of his wife (Eph. v. 23). Of Christ's headship of the Assembly the New Testament alone treats, and that only in the Epistles to the Ephesians and the Colossians. This is a much more circumscribed sphere, of course, than that of headship over the universe; but we are taught that it is He who is head over all things, whom God has given to the Church, which is His body, the fulness of Him who fills all in all. His relation to it, and by consequence its relation to Him, as viewed in this character, was both new and peculiar. Nothing of the kind had Israel, God's earthly people, ever known; nothing of the kind will they ever enjoy.

To the Church, whether viewed as His body or His

Bride, He is head, not Lord. Lord, of course He is; God made Him such (Acts ii. 36). Every knee in heaven, on earth, and under the earth (i. e., all intelligent creatures), must ever own Him as Lord (Phil. ii. 11). The Church, too, knows Him as the Lord; but He is head to, not Lord of, the Church. Headship and Lordship both belong to Him, but they are not convertible terms. As Lord, He stands out apart from all others; as head, He is in close association with that to which He is as such connected. Scripture, then, never speaks of Him as Lord in relation to the Church; for that clause in Eph. v. 29, when rightly read, stands thus: "Even as the Christ the Church."* Of this Assembly He is the head, and it stands to Him in a relation altogether new, being His body, the fulness of Him that filleth all in all. Paul alone, of the New Testament writers, treats of this branch of the subject, and to him was the truth of it first made known. The foundation on which the Assembly was to rest was announced, as we have seen, to Peter in the audience of the twelve. The existence of His body upon earth Christ first revealed to Paul (Eph. iii. 3) when in the company of his fellow-travelers, though in words they did not understand. The Lord Jesus was speaking to Saul, but He did not address them. How near were they to the Speaker from heaven, and yet remained strangers

---

* Attention to the phraseology of Scripture on this point will help us to form a judgment as to that disputed reading in Acts xx. 28, where many good authorities represent the apostle as having said "the Assembly of the Lord," instead of "the Assembly of God." The former reading we may dismiss as contrary to the phraseology and general teaching of Scripture. "Assembly of God" is a scriptural term; "Assembly of Christ" is a scriptural thought; "Assembly of the Lord," we believe, is neither the one nor the other.

to the communication embodied in that single sentence, "Why persecutest thou Me?" No question surely was ever asked more astounding to any one than this; no interrogation was ever addressed to a prisoner more condemnatory than this. From One whom Saul had never seen, and from that One in heavenly glory, the light of which the whole company beheld, came that startling, penetrating question to the impetuous opponent of God's saints. All that Saul was doing was known to his interrogator. What Saul was doing was unknown to himself. To turn aside the question was impossible; so personal it was, so heart-searching it must have been. To answer it satisfactorily was equally impossible. It convicted him of ignorance of God's mind, and of hatred to God and to His Son. Paul evidently never forgot it, nor the truth which by it was revealed. As proof that he never forgot it, we find that question recorded in all three accounts of his conversion, two of which are related by himself. Writing to the Corinthians, he tells them, too, of his sin (1 Cor. xv. 9). Exhorting the Philippians, he makes mention of it (iii. 6); and when unbosoming himself to his child in the faith, he again refers to it (1 Tim. i. 13). The truth, too, which was thus revealed took a firm hold of him. He taught it, he contended for it, he suffered for it (Eph. iii. 1). Further, by that question the Lord threw a shield over His persecuted ones, who were dear to Him, and arrested the arm of the self-constituted inquisitor of the saints. But He did more. By the form of His question He revealed the truth that His saints were part of Himself. Of old, Jehovah had declared of Israel that those who touched them touched the apple of His eye (Zech. ii. 8); i.e., that which a man guards most carefully. Here the Lord announced that in persecuting His saints Saul was persecuting Him. Thus the mystery was disclosed of a body upon earth which belonged to a head in heaven.

For teaching about this body we must turn, as we have said, to the Epistles of Paul; not that he was the only one who knew about it, for to God's holy apostles and prophets was it revealed by the Spirit (Eph. iii. 5); but to Paul was it first made known by revelation (Eph. iii. 3). A body on earth, its head in heaven, this constitutes the mystery of the Christ, the two making up the one mystic man—the Christ. And this body is His complement, or fulness, who fills all in all (Eph. i. 23). Without it, as the ascended Christ He was not complete; with it, there is nothing left to be desired. The divine conception of the Christ thus stands forth in all its completeness. But what a conception! His fulness the body is, who fills all in all; thoughts, statements, a revelation, we have about the Christ which far surpass our small intelligence to grasp in their fulness. This, however, is simple, and within the power of our mental faculties to take in, that great as is His glory, who is God as well as man, when looked at as man, though He fills the whole universe with His divine glory, He, the Christ, is not complete without His body, the Church. What an interest He must take, He does take, in that which stands in this relation to Him! It is His body. How close to Him! how really a part of Himself! How full of meaning, then, was the question, "Why persecutest thou Me?"

Now this body, in common in this respect with the Assembly of God, is presented in the Word in three different lights. All the saints, from Pentecost to the rapture of 1 Thess. iv. 16, 17, form part of it, and together compose it, according to Eph. i. 23, Col. i. 18. And although as saints they will reign with Christ, and as the Assembly, the Lamb's wife in glory, will be the metropolis of the Kingdom, the new Jerusalem, it would nevertheless appear, from the revelation of the body being His complement, who fills all in all, that this relation of the Church to Him, its head, will forever abide; for viewed as the risen man, He is not complete without it. The body, then, will not, like a dissolving view, merge into the Bride, the former disappearing when the latter is publicly displayed. These two characters of the Church are quite distinct now, and will be forever.

Again, all the saints upon earth at any one time between Pentecost and the rapture are viewed as the body of Christ. Of this we learn from Eph. iv. 16, Col. 2. 19. Hence, at no time of its existence upon earth does it ever lack a limb. It is never, as respects its members, defective. A maimed body, a defective body, forms no part of scripture-teaching about the Assembly or Church of God; and it should be noticed that only when Scripture treats of the body as wholly in existence upon earth, do we read of its members, or of its joints and bands. Without all its members it could not, of course, rightly grow, nor properly discharge its functions. But we are plainly taught that it should grow, and, as occasion requires, should act, and it is to do both upon earth. Hence it is regarded as at all times fully furnished with its members whilst here below. Had we simply man's thoughts about the body of Christ, we should probably have had it depicted as fully furnished with its members only when viewed in its most comprehensive character, embracing all the saints who do, or will, form part of it. This, however, is the only light in which, when viewed in the Word, the existence of its members is unnoticed. The wisdom of God in speaking of the members, when the body is looked at as on earth, all may discern. The absence of all mention of the members when the body is viewed as complete in glory, we may surely account for satisfactorily.

Further, each local assembly, meaning thereby all the saints in any given locality, has the characteristic in Scripture of Christ's body, σῶμα Χριστοῦ. (1 Cor. xii. 27). We must say it has this characteristic; for the language of the passage, by the omission of the definite article before the noun "body," whilst defining the character of the local assembly, excludes most carefully the thought of independency. The local assembly is charged with the responsibility which belongs to Christ's body. Yet it is not the body of Christ to the exclusion of any of the saints elsewhere; for the saints in any given place are really only part of the body of Christ, though, viewed in their local character, they are responsible to act for Christ as His body in that place. And whether they understand it or not, whether they act accordingly or not, Scripture regards all saints in any one place as together Christ's body, however many and diverse may be the names which they give to themselves. For there is but one body, as, of course, the head can have but one. Now this truth, when apprehended, deals a death-blow to any denominational position or association. "There is one body, and one Spirit" (Eph. iv. 4).

Of this body Christ is the head (Eph. iv. 15; Col. i. 18; ii. 19); and from Him as such, "all the body by joints and bands having nourishment ministered, and knit together, increaseth with the increase of God." One learns from the Word of a double work constantly going on. By the gifts from the ascended Christ, laborers in the word and doctrine (apostles, prophets, evangelists, pastors, and teachers), souls are reached, and the body edified. But, besides this, we are taught of another work, the increase of the body. For this the service of all the members is requisite, but in connection with and in subordination to the Head. "From whom the whole body fitly joined together, and compacted by that which every joint supplieth, according to the effectual working in the measure of every part, maketh increase of the body unto the edifying of itself in love" (Eph. iv. 16). Thus does the Head care for His body, and provide for its edification and growth. The body is to increase, and that according to the effectual working in the measure of each one part. Are all Christians alive to this? By the gifts of Christ souls are converted, the body is edified, the saints can be perfected (Eph. iv. 11, 12). The increase of the body, however, is only mentioned in connection with the proper working of each one part. Surely there is something here which is too much forgotten. Edification by gifts of ministry is generally understood. Is the increase of the body by the effectual working of each one part as generally acknowledged? Is it generally remembered that to "every one of us is given grace according to the measure of the gift of Christ" (Eph. iv. 7).

Now, were this the case, would there not be a marked difference in the outward aspect of the Church of God? Instead of casting all responsibility of the assembly on those who labor in the Word, which has too generally been done, being content just to receive from such what they may have to give, would there not be more real fellowship and a more general care for the increase of the body? Now, where this is forgotten, can it be said that Christians have entered in a broad, catholic way into that which interests Christ upon earth? Are any contented with seeking their own profit merely? Are any satisfied with, in addition to that, helping on the spread of the gospel of God's grace? A happy, blessed service that surely is: but is that all that is put before us in the New Testament? Are we desirous of, and helping forward as far as we can, the increase of the body of Christ? Has the truth of the increase of the body, by the effectual working of each one part, dawned upon the reader, if a Christian, as that which very closely concerns him?

There is a circle of interest very dear to God, within the limits of which the whole race of man upon earth is included. This the Lord Jesus set forth, after He was risen from the dead, when He commissioned His disciples to preach repentance and remission of sins among all nations, beginning at Jerusalem. Nothing less extensive than this for evangelistic work should bound the sympathies and desires of God's saints. There is, however, another circle of interest, less extensive in its limits, yet not less important, and very dear to Christ. Within its range none but true Christians are numbered. It is the body of Christ, the increase of which He desires, and in the work of which each part of the body should take its part. Again we would ask, Has the reader acknowledged his responsibility in connection with it?

The lack of apprehension as regards this is, however, of no recent date. Denominational differences have but fostered it and strengthened it. The language, too, of men, accepted as perfectly proper, bears witness to it, as they talk of "this cause," "that cause," or "our cause." Yet, however widely extended may be the cause for which they plead, or which they support, it is far less comprehensive than that of the body of Christ. But to a much older date than that of Luther and Calvin must we trace back this evil. For we see it in those communities in which the clergy are looked upon as the church, and in which they arrogate to themselves all church action and authority. Herein they are wrong. Those who minister the Word are not the church, though part of it. The distinction between those who minister and those who do not is perfectly scriptural, but delegating to the clergy all church power and action, resulting, very probably, from the decline of spirituality in early days, this it is which has deadened the sense of general responsibility in reference to the increase of the body, till what Scripture teaches upon it has been wholly and for centuries forgotten.

The question, then, may be asked, What am I to do? How can I contribute to the increase of the body? The Head, we would reply, will surely teach each member what is its place in the body. To Him we should look for direction; for it is His body, and He knows the part which each can take for the increase of the whole. How often have Christians looked to men for guidance as to their line of service! How often have godly men set others to work, instead of leaving that to the wisdom of the Head, thus practically ignoring the Head! Brotherly counsel is one thing, human direction is another. Apollos, as the servant of Christ, would not be directed even by Paul. Paul acknowledged the freedom of the workman from human control.

But if we have to own failure in so little apprehending scripture-teaching about the body of Christ, if from the natural selfishness of the human heart we have hitherto restricted our interest to a range less extensive than that of Christ's body, the Head, we have to thank God, has never ceased to care for anything less than all His members. And His unwearied devotedness is seen afresh in recalling the attention of His people to important and practical truths so long forgotten. How small, how narrow, how contracted, are men's thoughts compared with the revelation of the body on earth united to the Head in heaven! What it is to have such a Head, and who that Head is, the apostle Paul dwells upon in the Epistle to the Colossians. What becomes of those who are members of the body is specially set forth in that to the Ephesians. To a study of these Epistles under the teaching of the Holy Ghost we recommend any who desire full instruction on the subject.

Nothing can be closer to Christ than the being a member of His body. A privilege indeed; but a privilege connected with great responsibilities. As thus connected with Him, sectional distinctions should drop, and denominational position be surrendered. As members one of another, there are responsibilities likewise. On these we hope to touch in a future article. Meanwhile we here close for the present, hoping in our next to look at the Church as the bride of Christ.

CHAPTER V.

THE BRIDE OF CHRIST.

AS the Assembly of Christ, the Church is told of its everlasting security; as His body, it is reminded of its responsibility; as His bride, it even now enjoys in a special manner His love; "for Christ loved the Church, and gave Himself for it" (Eph. v. 25). To her *present* position of bride the attention of the reader is requested.

The appellation of bride, used of the Church, is only met with in the Apocalypse (xxi. 9; xxii. 17), in which book she is also called the Lamb's wife (xix. 7; xxi. 9). She is the bride of the Lamb, and to Him only, of course, does she stand in this position, to be openly manifested as such, after that which professes to be the Church shall have been publicly judged as the great whore (Rev. xix. 2), the Babylon of the Apocalypse. Now from three of the New Testament penmen do we learn about the Church in this special connection with Christ. Of her beauty in the Lamb's eyes Matthew tells us; of Christ's care and service, to make her answer to the desire of His heart, Paul informs us. To John was it permitted to behold in vision something of her personal glory, when she shall be displayed to the world as the bride, the Lamb's wife. Now such teaching is peculiar to the New Testament. No Old Testament prophet ever touched upon this theme. No Old Testament poet ever descanted upon such a union; yet David was inspired to sing of the King's consort (Psa. xlv.); Solomon composed the "Song of songs;"

Isaiah described the future glory and greatness of her to whom Jehovah will be a husband (liv.). These inspired men, however, were occupied with something very different from the Church of God. A little attention will make this clear.

Isaiah makes plain that it is of Jerusalem he writes (liv.), to which Jehovah formerly acted as husband (Ezek. xvi. 8–14), till forced to cast her off for a time for her whoredom with the nations, her lovers. Having learnt to her sorrow what widowhood and shame are, she will by and by enjoy restoration to divine favor, and be publicly reinstated in her proper relation to Him who is Israel's King and her husband. It was of this bright future that David sung when he penned that "song of loves" (Psa. xlv.), in which the queen is introduced, and described as accompanied by her virginal train, when she has received from the King the place of honor, and her favor is to be sought after by the rich among the people.

But is not the Church, it may be asked, made mention of in this psalm? Heavenly saints, who form it, are expressly noticed therein, though as quite distinct from the queen. They are just touched upon under the term "His fellows" (ver. 7), among whom, as Heb. iii. 14 in the original makes plain, we must include all those who are now saints upon earth, believers on the Lord Jesus Christ. The "fellows" of the King must be very different from the queen. Both, indeed, have to do with Him who is the King, though clearly distinct the one from the other.

Of Jerusalem's past and future the prophetic word instructs us. Her restoration to favor, and to her proper position before all the earth, the prophet Isaiah predicts, and the psalmist graphically depicts. But for this to be righteously effected there must be the moral restoration of the remnant of the people. Now it is of this Solomon writes in the Canticles, the purport of which, briefly expressed, is to show the pains taken by the Beloved to get hold afresh of the full affection of His loved one;* for the two are not described therein as meeting for the first time. Canticles, then, does not set forth the intercourse of the Church with Christ. The Church is not mentioned in the Song of songs, though Christ is prominent in the book, and the affection of His heart toward His earthly people is beautifully set forth. Yet there is much instruction for the individual Christian in that unique composition of the son of David; and many a believer, tasting of the unwearied love of Christ, after he has wandered in heart from Him, has found therein language just suited to him as a saint. The Church's position, however, in reference to Christ, and His dealings with her, are very different from both the one and the other as set forth in that book.

For all teaching, then, about the Church as the bride of Christ, we must turn to the New Testament. To that let us now direct our attention.

On the shore of the lake of Galilee, in the audience of the multitude, the Lord spake the parables of the sower, the tares, the mustard tree, and the leaven. Inside the house, when alone with His disciples, He expounded the parable of the tares, and gave to them in addition those

---

* For though Jerusalem, not the nation, is the queen, Jehovah will stand to the nation also, as He has done once, in the relation of her husband (Hosea ii. 16-20). So, before Jerusalem can have her place of honor by the King's side, the remnant of the people must be restored in heart to Him from whom they have revolted. Canticles describes Christ dealing with hearts. Isa. liv., Psa. xlv. acquaint us with Jerualem's future glory.

of the treasure, the pearl, and the net (Matt. xiii. 1–52). The outward character of the Kingdom of the Heavens, as men would see it, the Lord spake in parables to the multitude. Its aspect from God's point of view He reserved for the special information of His disciples. They, and they only, were then permitted to learn what a treasure His saints were to Him, what a beautiful thing the Church would be in His eyes, and how He would care for His own people—symbolized by the good fish—through the instrumentality of His ministering servants. For the reader will remark that in the parable of the net the good fish only are cared for; in the supplementary remarks the bad fish only are dealt with. On that occasion, in the house, it was disclosed for the first time that there should be an object of surpassing beauty in the eyes of Christ, which He would die to possess. He would buy the field for the sake of the treasure concealed in it; but He would purchase the pearl for its own preciousness.

Seeking goodly pearls, the merchantman is arrested in his search by the sight of one pearl of great price. His search is stopped; he goes no further; he desires nothing more. Pearls he was seeking for; one pearl, when found, has satisfied his heart's desire. To possess it is now all his aim. He has valued it, and valued it aright. What is that value? Who shall determine it? Who shall give the price? One alone does that—the merchantman himself. He went, we read, and sold all that he had, and bought it. Its value to him is attested by that which he gives to possess it; for he must possess it. In plain language, Christ would die to possess that one pearl. It is of His death, then, that He here makes mention; and it is in these two parables that the Lord in this chapter speaks of His death. Other scriptures acquaint us with the atoning character of His death. These parables acquaint us with another reason why He died. He wanted to acquire the treasure; He desired to possess the pearl. How precious, then, to Him, how satisfying to His eye and heart is the one pearl of great price, for which, in order to purchase it, He has given up all that He had, speaking of Himself here, of course, as a man. The language of Scripture, we must remember, is definite; no waste of words do we find in that book. Whenever, then, we meet with epithets, we may be sure that there is force in them. So here let the reader note the language of Christ Himself: one pearl of *great price* ($\pi o \lambda \acute{u} \tau \iota \mu o \nu$). No mere man surely would ever have dared thus to characterize the Church. Many and many a saint has heartily, truly declared that Christ is to them the chiefest among ten thousand; but Christ by this epithet tells us what His Church is in His eyes. Of the Church's affection for Christ we read elsewhere; but in the parable, and in Eph. v., it is His estimate of her, and His love to her that is dwelt upon. What her joy will be might be conceived; what His delight in her would be, had need to be revealed—and that He Himself first touches upon it.

Passing from the parable to the doctrinal teaching of Eph. v., where Paul writes of the Church in its spousal relation to Christ, we are taught of His love to her, the way in which He has shown it, proves it still, and will yet manifest it. But, as is often the case in Scripture, the Spirit of God, whilst touching upon what has already been revealed, adds to its fulness. The parable described Christ giving up all He had to possess the pearl. The Holy Ghost, in the Ephesians, speaks in language, if possible, yet more full. For the apostle wrote, "Christ loved the Church, and gave *Himself* for it" (Eph. v. 25). All that He could give for it, all that He can be to it, she is assured of in these words.

A pearl of great price! But who would have discovered that? who, looking around on the Church of God, remembering the sadly-blotted history it possesses, surveying what it is at present, who, indeed, would ever have discovered that it was a pearl, that it had any beauty, and that it was an object of great price? To bring this out, to make manifest its beauty and preciousness, Christ has and does minister to it.

We should mark the progressive stages of His service which the apostle traces out for us. First, Christ gave Himself for the Assembly. He died to possess the Church, and that because He loved it. The motive, the reason for thus dying, was simply the love of His heart. The parable tells us He desired to purchase it. The teaching of Ephesians acquaints us with the secret motive—love for it. His service for the Assembly did not, however, end there. Man's devotedness can proceed no further than to die instead of his object; but, in dying, man loses any earthly object. Christ, on the contrary, died to possess the Assembly, and His service for the object of His heart begins where that of a mere man's must end. So, secondly, He sanctifies and cleanses it with the washing of water by the Word. As first possessed, then, by Him, it does not answer to that which He desires. A pearl it is in His eyes, but He must bring out its beauty. This He does by the application of the Word. Once it was not His, but He bought it. It was not clean, so He would cleanse it. It was not set apart, but He would sanctify it. These are tokens of His love to His Assembly. By and by He will present the Assembly to Himself glorious, not having spot or wrinkle, or any such thing. Such is the end He has in view. What a service He has undertaken! What an end has He proposed to Himself! What delight will He have when He presents the Assembly to Himself glorious, without any blemish! Throughout this passage, the reader should remark, we have nothing told us of the Church's joy. Christ's love, Christ's present service, the end He has in view, on these points the Holy Ghost delights to dwell.

What a condition must the Assembly be in when He has to sanctify and cleanse it (or, as some would translate, "having cleansed it,") by the washing of water by the Word!—a plain declaration that it is not what He wants; yet He will not rest till He has made it all He desires. But more, He "nourisheth and cherisheth it" (ver. 29). All that it needs in its spousal relation to Him He supplies. To make it conformable to His desire, He applies to it the Word. Besides this, He ministers to it all that it wants. Nourishing and cherishing! What grace is there in that! Giving Himself for it, sanctifying it, cleansing it! What grace, too, in all this!

Viewed as man views the Assembly, could we say that it has requited such care and love? How little have those who form part of it had intelligence as to that which Christ is doing! There was surely a time in the history of every believer whose eye may light on this page, when salvation from wrath was desired, and perhaps known, but Church relationship to Christ unknown, or ignored. Can all the readers of this paper say that such is no longer true of them?

Unchanged, however, is Christ's estimate of the Assembly's worth. What the parable sets forth, His constant service on its behalf confirms. Yet how soon had He to tell one assembly that it had left its first love, and to charge another with having in its midst that doctrine which He hated! (Rev. ii. 15, compared with ver. 6). How early in the history of the Church had Jezebel been allowed a footing in that which bore His name, and He Himself had to stand without, knocking, to learn as it were whether there was in the assembly at Laodicea one heart faithful to Him! This personal ministration of Christ testified to the unchanging affection of His heart (Rev. iii. 19), and evidenced that He well knew the condition and position of His people, and most truly desired their welfare.

But this was in the past. Is He *still* unchanged? Those surely who have learnt in these days truth about the Church so long neglected, and even forgotten, can testify that His love and service are as unwearied as ever. Blessed for them that it is so. For what must those who form part of it be by nature, when, to enforce the observance by the husband of his duty and bearing towards his wife, the love of Christ and His service to the Church is set forth as a fitting illustration. What creatures, to need such an exhortation! How richly blest to be objects of Christ's love!

By and by His object will be accomplished. His present service to the Assembly will cease only because it will not be required, and He will present it to Himself glorious, answering to His wish about it. At this point, however, we must pass from the writings of Paul to those of John. Paul has set forth Christ's love to the Church, and told even an assembly of its relation to Christ, as representing locally the Bride (2 Cor. xi. 2). John writes of the time when the marriage of the Lamb shall have come (Rev. xix. 7); but the actual marriage he never describes. For, like the inside of the Father's house, it is essentially a scene fit only for heaven, and never therefore disclosed to the view of men on earth. We hear of the marriage of the Lamb. We are shown the Bride, the Lamb's wife, after the marriage, when displayed to earth; but her presentation to Him is carefully hidden from us. Heaven rejoices at it, we learn. Blessed, too, we are told, will those be who are called to the marriage supper of the Lamb (Rev. xix. 7–9). Here again all is looked at from the Lamb's point of view, not from that of the Bride. It is the fulfilment of His long-cherished desire that the great multitude unanimously announce. What her feelings will be, John was not directed here to declare.

We do, however, gather from his writings something of her feelings toward Christ; for when He announces Himself, at the end of the Revelation, as the root and offspring of David, and the bright and Morning Star, an immediate response is made to Him by the Spirit and the Bride, who, both addressing Him, say, "Come." Her desire is to see Him. She wishes for His return. She asks Him to come. That is the voice of the Church as a whole. When it was in its pristine condition, one could have fancied the whole Assembly, with one heart and voice, uttering that word "Come." In the present condition of the Assembly that cannot be done. Some there are, really part of the body of Christ, who understand not the truth of the Lord's return. Some, too, have taken the place of being Christians—are such in name, but in name only. How could they join in that cry? Are souls, then, to be deprived of the opportunity and joy of echoing that cry to Him, the Morning Star, by reason of the present condition of the Assembly upon the earth? By no means; for the Word immediately adds, "Let him that heareth say, Come." God thus provides that even in the disorderly condition of the Church souls should be allowed to welcome the coming of Christ.

Not only does the Bride, however, desire His return; for we read in Rev. xix. 7 of the Bride, when the marriage day has come, having made herself ready, being adorned for her Husband. And her bridal attire, how simple it is, yet how comely! "To her was granted that she should be arrayed in fine linen clean and white: for the fine linen is the righteous deeds of the saints" (Rev. xix. 8). What a contrast to that of the great whore, who is described as clothed in purple and scarlet, with ornaments of gold, precious stones, and pearls! (Rev. xvii. 4.) On the person of the whore was seen that which attracts and pleases the natural eye. On the Bride was just that which would please the Bridegroom's eyes—the righteousnesses ($\delta\iota\varkappa\alpha\iota\omega\mu\alpha\tau\alpha$) of the saints—it is what they have done, indeed, yet all the fruit of divine grace, and of the energizing power of the Holy Ghost. The whore delights in meretricious splendor; the Bride is arrayed in that which witnesses of grace bestowed on her. The Bride, too, is the pearl of great price in Christ's eyes. No need, then, could she have to deck out her person with pearls, etc. Such an attire, such ornaments, would only dim instead of enhancing her beauty in His eyes. Gold, pearls, precious stones—these speak of God as Creator. He made them. Righteousnesses of saints— these are the fruits of that new creation, of which Christ is the beginning, and in which all who form the Bride have their part. The significance of her clothing we can all, therefore, understand.

But observe, the marriage is not described as taking place immediately on the rapture of the saints. In Rev. v. they are seen in heaven already. It is not till chap. xix. that the marriage day is spoken of as having come. Then she will be found ready. Till the rapture she can say to Him, "Come." But throughout all this time she proves His love and care. Her beauty He discerned at the outset. His love and service to her make it manifest; and when the time arrives for the marriage, He who has nourished her, cleansed her and sanctified her, will find her prepared for Him. His service to her, it will then be seen, has not been in vain.

CHAPTER VI.

ITS RELATION TO THE HOLY GHOST.

IN treating of the Assembly of God, we must remember the work of the Holy Ghost in connection with it. But how different are the relations of the Holy Ghost to the Assembly from those of God, and of Christ! It is God's Assembly, it is Christ's body, but in no sense does it bear the Holy Ghost's name; yet without the Spirit's work, and that not only in converting power, the Assembly would have no existence. To understand, then, scripture teaching about the Church, we must acknowledge the scripture doctrine of the Father, the Son, and the Holy Ghost—three persons, yet but one God. For the Assembly, which is the Church of the living God, is in God the Father (1 Thess. i. 1); has for its foundation the truth of the person of Christ as the Son of the living God (Matt. xvi. 16, 18); and is indwelt by the Holy Ghost, thereby becoming the habitation of God (Eph. ii. 22). God, in the person of the Holy Ghost, has by His indwelling presence made it His temple (1 Cor. iii. 16).

Further, the presence of the Holy Ghost in the Assembly is constant and unconditional. Till the Lord Jesus Christ went on high to the Father, the Holy Ghost could not come thus to abide on earth (John xvi. 7). After Christ had ascended, the Holy Ghost came on the day of Pentecost, and has ever since dwelt in the Assembly of God here below. Ananias and Sapphira learnt the reality of His presence when Peter, charging home on them their sin, told the man that he had lied to the Holy

Ghost, and asked the woman why they had agreed to tempt the Spirit of the Lord (Acts v. 3, 9). The assembly at Antioch proved the truth of His presence when He told them to separate unto Him Barnabas and Saul for the work to which He had called them (Acts xiii. 2). The Lord, too, had announced beforehand that when the Holy Ghost came, He would abide with the disciples forever (John xiv. 16); and the Spirit's response, with that of the Bride, to the Lord's announcement that He is the Morning Star, demonstrates that the divine prediction has indeed come to pass. The Spirit is with the Assembly forever; so that it will never, whilst on earth, be deprived of His presence. He dwells, it is true, in each believer; but He dwells in the whole Assembly as well.

These truths are quite distinct. They must not be confounded; nor should the one be held without the other. The difference, too, between them is very marked; for the Holy Ghost, as dwelling in each believer, makes that saint's body His temple. But as dwelling in the Assembly, the Assembly becomes the temple of God. A temple of the Holy Ghost is the body of each believer; the temple of God is the Assembly of God upon earth. Whilst stating all this, it should, however, be clearly understood that the Spirit of God had been, throughout all ages since man was created, working upon earth. From the commencement of the book of Genesis to the close of Revelation, the Holy Ghost is seen having to do with earth and with men. Yet never, till the last time that the feast of Pentecost was observed according to God's mind, did the Spirit take up His abode on earth as the third person of the Godhead, forming a habitation, a temple in which He dwells. This is Christian truth, and distinctive Christian truth; for as He did not dwell on earth before the cross, so He will not dwell on it after the rapture. Constantly working before the cross, He will as certainly work on earth after the rapture of the saints, but will not dwell here as He does now. To be poured upon all flesh is one thing; to dwell in a temple on earth is another.

Till after the exodus of Israel from Egypt, God never dwelt upon earth. He first dwelt in the tabernacle. He dwelt, too, in the temple, until Nebuchadnezzar came to destroy it. From that time God did not dwell on earth till the Lord Jesus Christ entered this world as a babe, at the hour when men, for the most part, were wrapt in slumber. "In Him dwelleth all the fulness of the Godhead bodily" (Col. ii. 9). Created things, animate and inanimate, acknowledged His presence and power by obeying His word. The fishes in the sea, the wind and the waves, were subservient to His will. But His presence here was but for a time, and that a very limited one. He died, and left earth, no longer to be found dwelling upon it.

For a very brief period it was again true that God was not dwelling on this globe. But when the day of Pentecost had fully come, this earth became once more a dwelling-place for God in the person of the Holy Ghost, who has never been absent from it for a single moment since that sound as of a rushing mighty wind was heard, which filled all the house in which the disciples of Christ were sitting in Jerusalem (Acts ii. 2). God had come to earth to dwell on it for the third time in the world's history. How favored is this earth! A globe so small, yet God's habitation is found on it!

The fact noticed as to the Spirit's coming is instructive and significant. He filled all the house, but He did not fill all Jerusalem. He was upon earth, but He did not then dwell in every part of it. In that house He was that morning, but He was not in the temple on mount Moriah. The building which the Lord entered as God's house at Jerusalem was never part of God's habitation in the Spirit. The majestic structure of the temple never received as its occupant God the Holy Ghost; and though He came that morning to dwell on earth, He did not fill the world with His presence. In like manner the habitation of God as it at present exists, though reaching far beyond the bounds of the nation of Israel, has nevertheless limits which fall considerably short of the boundaries of this terrestrial globe. It had limits on that day when the Holy Ghost filled the house, but did not fill Jerusalem. It had limits in apostolic times; it has limits still. It is true that no individual upon earth need remain outside of them, on either natural or moral grounds, if the grace of God reaches the heart, and the conscience is dealt with. Souls from amongst the Hottentots and the Esquimaux, the South Sea Islanders and the red Indians, as well as from among the most refined and intellectual members of civilized society, can each and all form part of God's habitation in the Spirit; for God now commands all men everywhere to repent; and if any man enters in by Christ (the door), he is saved (John x. 9), and finds himself a member of the Assembly of God.

Yet it is a fact that the Assembly does not embrace within its limits every soul dwelling upon earth, and indeed it was never intended so to do: God is visiting the Gentiles to take out of them a people for His name (Acts xv. 14). He is saving now a remnant according to the election of grace, in contradistinction to the saving of all Israel by and by (Rom. xi. 5, 26). The conversion of all

ITS RELATION TO THE HOLY GHOST. 61

the world is not the divine purpose during the absence of Christ from earth. The limits of the Assembly are formed by those in whom the Holy Ghost dwells. There is a *within* and a *without*, as expressed in God's word, which, when using such language, has reference to the confines of the Assembly of God. "Walk in wisdom," we are told, "toward them that are without" (Col. iv. 5). "That ye may walk honestly toward them that are without" (1 Thess. iv. 12). Again, writes the apostle, "What have I to do to judge them also that are without? do not ye judge them that are within? But them that are without God judgeth" (1 Cor. v. 12, 13). Within, the Holy Ghost dwells; without, Satan, who is the god and prince of this world, exercises sway.

But besides dwelling in the Assembly, which thus becomes God's habitation, God's temple, the Holy Ghost has also formed the body of Christ. "By one Spirit are we all baptized into one body, whether we be Jews or Gentiles, whether we be bond or free; and have been all made to drink into one Spirit" (1 Cor. xii. 13). It is by the baptism of the Holy Ghost that the body of Christ is formed, to which we have already directed the attention of our readers. This was effected at Pentecost for those who had been Jews; and Gentiles were first brought into the body by sharing in this baptism in the house of Cornelius. And Paul, as we here read, though he was not converted on the day of Pentecost, neither was present at Cæsarea when Peter visited the Roman centurion, yet shared in that baptism, as did all the Corinthian saints to whom he wrote; for *saints only* can share in it. Saints only can be members of the body of Christ, united to Him by the Holy Ghost, though the Spirit dwells in the Assembly in which there may be some who are only professors (1 Cor. iii. 17).

In the body of Christ so formed neither national nor social distinctions exist. Baptized by one Spirit, the unity of the Spirit of Eph. iv. 3 is called into existence. Having all been made to drink into one Spirit, the unity should be acknowledged and manifested, and the scriptural way of manifesting it is by breaking bread as the Lord has appointed it (1 Cor. x. 17). Whatever would practically deny the oneness of the body of Christ we are clearly to turn from; and it should be remembered that the divinely appointed way of showing it is by our presence at the Lord's table. As of the *new creation* in Christ, all distinctions cease. But this does not affect the distinctions in the Church; for there are distinctions in the Assembly. In Christ we are all one. In the Assembly there are the overseers and the overseen. In the body there are the members, each having its own functions. In 1 Cor. xii. 14–26, the apostle, taking as his illustration the natural body, sets forth *four* points of great practical value.

First we can never, if part of the body, be removed from it. It is God who has put us there, according to His own will. "If the ear shall say, Because I am not the eye, I am not of the body; is it therefore not of the body?" The members have no choice about it. They are in the body, they are part of the body. Just so it is with Christians and the body of Christ. They may be ignorant of it, they may refuse to learn about it, *but they cannot get out of their place in the body*. For as none but true Christians are members of the body of Christ, none such can be lost; the body of Christ will be found perfect in the end. In the body they are, and to it they ever belong. But the body is one: two bodies united to one head is contrary to all order in creation. So with the body of Christ; there is one body, as there is one Head. But here the common thoughts and language of Christians are at variance with God's truth. Bodies of Christians men speak of, and approve of: *one* body is all that God owns, and all that Scripture teaches. If Scripture is to teach us, we must own only one body, and so be on true Church ground, on which all Christians, if simply in subjection to the Word, can meet; and once there, we must stay there. Thus the foot cannot get free from the body, whatever it may say about it; no more can Christians shake themselves free of their responsibility to acknowledge and maintain practically the truth of the oneness of the body of Christ.

Secondly, we must ever remember that one member does not constitute the body. "If they were all one member, where were the body? But now are they many members, yet but one body." For one member, then, in the body of Christ to arrogate to itself the functions of the body must be clearly wrong. Wherever that is done, the individual so acting, if in self-will, is wrong; if with the cordial agreement of others, is both wrong himself, and those who allow it are abetting and fostering the evil. But is this understood?

Thirdly, we cannot do without every member. "The eye cannot say unto the hand, I have no need of thee: nor, again, the head to the feet, I have no need of you. Nay, much more those members of the body which seem to be more feeble are necessary." It may be, and it surely is the case, that from the disorder in the Assembly of God we cannot avail ourselves of the help of every member of the body of Christ; but for our part, though deprived in a great measure of their assistance and service, we cannot without suffering loss be independent of one of them; so closely are the members of the body bound up with one another. But all this denominationalism ignores, and thereby robs the whole Church of that which has been provided for the benefit of all. How little is this seen! The Corinthians, when split up into parties, were robbing themselves of the gifts given for them all (1 Cor. iii. 21–23). How suicidal to the Church's best interest is her advocacy of denominational ground!

Lastly, God sets the members in the body as it hath pleased Him. None, therefore, can choose their place, though each may have to learn what it is. But, reminded of this, all envying of another's place, all imitation of another's service, should be carefully guarded against. Each has his own place, each his own service, which, if rightly carried out, will conduce to the healthy increase of the whole body. What a busy hive the assembly at Rome must have been, judging from the remarks on individuals made by the apostle in the last chapter of his epistle to that assembly! All the service there enumerated might not be what men call great, but it was true, and accepted of God.

Most practical is the truth of the oneness of the body of Christ. Formed by the baptism of the Holy Ghost, that oneness exists now on earth. May each one who forms part of it, discovering his place, and the character of his service in the body and in the Assembly, keep the one and perform the other.

CHAPTER VII.

OF WHOM COMPOSED.

WHEN the Lord Jesus Christ was upon earth He spoke of His Assembly as then non-existent. He had not yet built it (Matt. xvi. 18). Till the Holy Ghost came, consequent on His ascension, it was not, and could not be formed. The Spirit's presence, therefore, inaugurated a new era. By the baptism of the Holy Ghost the body of Christ was called into being (1 Cor. xii. 13). No Old Testament saint then, could have been a member of the Church, or Assembly of God, which is the body of Christ. In the Kingdom of God every one of them will be found, when the Lord Jesus Christ comes in power and great glory. But part of the Church of God they never were, nor, we can add, ever will be; for in heaven, as well as upon earth, the Church is viewed as distinct from the worthies of old.

This we are taught in the epistle to the Hebrews, and the point is an important one to keep before the mind; for unless the great landmarks of Scripture are known, and dispensational teaching is apprehended, we cannot rightly divide the Word of truth (2 Tim. ii. 15). How such a thought should make one careful in the putting forth of truth, as well as diligent in acquiring an understanding of it! The Word of truth should be rightly divided. The apostle gently intimates by this remark to his child in the faith, that unless the workman was careful he might fail to do it. With Paul, then, the unfolding of Scripture was not the giving out of man's opinion upon it. It could be rightly divided; yet, unless Timothy was careful, that might not always be the case.

Now, important as it is for us to be taught correctly about the Church of God, it was of all importance for those in apostolic times, who, formerly Jews, were such no longer, in order that they should clearly see how distinct was their proper Christian position from that which they had previously prized, and with which they had been associated. To such Paul wrote in Hebrews xii. 22-24. Going forth to Christ without the camp, they would surrender much which they had previously valued, and valued very highly. Would they be losers thereby? To answer such a question he introduces his readers to a millennial scene, and lays open to their gaze the court of heaven, arranged, so to speak, in the order of precedence, and shows the connection between the earthly seat of the Kingdom and the real metropolis of the universe; "Ye are come unto mount Sion; and unto the city of the living God, the heavenly Jerusalem; and to an innumerable company of angels, a general assembly; and to the Church of the first-born, which are written in heaven; and to God the Judge of all; and to the spirits of just men made perfect; and to Jesus the mediator of the new covenant; and to the blood of sprinkling, that speaketh better things than that of Abel" (*rather*, better than Abel). To all this they then come, though in spirit only as yet. Thus, that to which the Jews in millennial days never will attain, what the earthly people never can have, was theirs, who from amongst them had confessed the Lord Jesus, theirs really, though not then enjoyed. All that they had come to the apostle enumerates, but marks off each thing distinctly from the rest by the conjunction "and." The position therefore of the Church in heaven this passage points out. The Assembly of the first-born ones (πρωτοτόκων), as the Holy Ghost here designates them, is seen next to God on His one hand, and the Old Testament saints—the spirits of just men made perfect— are seen as equally near to Him on the other; but two distinct companies never amalgamated. Both are equally near to God (that we must ever remember); but the Church of the first-born ones and the Old Testament saints are described as separated companies in heaven, each having their own proper position on high.

Who then, it may be asked, form the Church of the first-born ones? Some formerly Jews, and some formerly Gentiles; for the Scripture recognizes three classes as at present existing upon earth—the Jews, the Gentiles, and the Church of God (1 Cor. x. 32). Before the cross there were but two classes—the Jews and the Gentiles. By-and-by there will again be but two upon earth, when the word by Moses shall have its accomplishment: "Rejoice, O ye nations, with His people" (Deut. xxxii. 43). At present there exists also the third—the Church of God.

To this company the Lord made reference in John x. 16, when He announced the formation of the one flock under the care and the guardianship of the one Shepherd; for the reader should mark the Lord's language. One *flock* He speaks of, (ποίμνη), to be composed of the sheep in Israel, whom He was about to lead out of the *fold* (αὐλή), and of the sheep from amongst the Gentiles, who were never in it. This flock then was something quite new, and unthought of, till the Lord taught men about it. Observe, that to make the one flock, He first leads out of the fold those which had been in it. It was not the bringing those formerly Gentiles on to Jewish ground that He had here in view. That in its full sense never was done, and never will be done. It was not making proselytes to Judaism of Gentiles who harkened to His teaching. That the Lord never did. The time too for that, in accordance with God's thoughts, was then passing away. What the Lord treats of is the getting the two companies, who were to form the one flock, on to new ground altogether. The flock therefore of which He speaks could not be formed, till God dealt with Gentiles in grace equally with Jews. From the days of Abraham to the cross God was acting in a different manner. None therefore, who died before the cross, could form part of the one flock, the Assembly, or Church of God.

Years after we get this truth of the component parts of the flock affirmed by different apostles. James, in the council at Jerusalem, endorsed Peter's statement, that God had visited the Gentiles, to take out of them a people for His name (Acts xv. 14). Later on, Paul, writing to the Romans, bore witness that there was, from among Israel, "a remnant according to the election of grace" (Rom. xi. 5). The apostle of the circumcision spoke of believers from amongst the Gentiles. The apostle of the Gentiles acknowledged the presence in the Assembly of some who had once been Jews. But, both Peter and Paul distinctly pointed out, that it was only an election from the one and from the other. Those from the Gentiles did not become Jews; those from amongst the Jews did not become part of the one flock by virtue of their descent according to the flesh. Yet there is but one flock, one Assembly—"God's flock," as Peter calls it (1 Peter v. 2, 3), "God's Church," as Paul designates it (Acts xx. 28). Both terms, it will be seen, are instructive, attesting to whom those comprising the flock and Assembly belong, even God, but without referring to their former condition, whether moral or dispensational.

The truth, therefore, was owned by Peter as well as by Paul, though it is only in the writings of the latter that we find it dwelt on, and treated doctrinally.

At the end of the first chapter of the Ephesians, Paul introduces the subject of the Church of God, when writing of the present place on high of Him who is its Head. In the second chapter he developes the subject, and shows us who those are that compose it; first setting forth what they had been morally (vers. 1–10), and then what had been their condition dispensationally (vers. 11–22). Morally, nothing could have been more hopeless; spiritually dead, they had required quickening power to be put forth on their behalf by God for them to live. How wholly were they, one and all, dependent on the love, and mercy, and favor of God! For if they needed quickening power to be put forth by God that they should live, the putting forth of that power depended solely on the activity of God in grace. But what a comfort to remember the class of persons morally on whose behalf He thus acts. Dispensationally, the Jews had been nigh, and the Gentiles had been far off. The former had thus occupied a vantage-ground, which the latter had not. That vantage-ground has disappeared, for the Church: for those once far off, are in Christ made nigh by His blood; and those once Jews, with those once Gentiles, are created one new man in Christ—a new relationship in Christ which had never existed before, the twain made one in Christ. Learning this, we should not, it is clear, look to the Old Testament for instruction as to the formation of the Church, nor for guidance as to its worship. It did not exist in those days, nor was there anything like it ever called into being. Nothing analogous to it can be traced in the pages of the Hebrew writers. Any incorporation then of Jewish practices with Christian worship should have been sedulously guarded against, and that which the New Testament teaches about the Church, the new man, the body of Christ, should have been sought out and conformed to. Has this been generally done?

But is there not, some may ask, anything in the Old Testament which refers to the Church? Surely there is. For, although its then future existence was not made known, we can trace in the pages of the Hebrew Scriptures typical teaching about it, both as the bride of Christ, and as formed of believers from Jews and from Gentiles. There are personages in the Old Testament history who shadow forth in some way or other the Lord Jesus Christ. Of these we would here mention but two, Isaac and Solomon; the former, the type of the Lord as the risen one, and the heir of all things that belong to His Father; the latter as King of peace, and the King's Son who sits upon the throne of David. To Isaac Rebekah was brought as his bride, but not till Abraham had received him back as it were from the dead. Solomon had a bride—Pharaoh's daughter—connected in the closest way with the king, yet distinct from Israel, and who lived in a house prepared for her by her husband. She had part with him, yet was apart from Israel. Isaac with his wife, and Solomon with his, are both typical of Christ and the Church. The former shadows out that it is, as risen, Christ has His bride. The latter delineates the King's Son in His royal state in connection with Israel, yet in the closest possible way connected also with one who has no part with the earthly people of God.

Besides this, we can trace out in Leviticus xxiii. some-

OF WHOM COMPOSED. 71

thing of the peculiar composition of the Church which we have been considering. The feasts of the Lord therein described were important elements of Judaism; and Moses in three out of the five books which bear his name, dwells at some length on them. In Deuteronomy xvi. he describes the character of each of the three great feasts, as he sets forth the spirit in which they were severally to be observed. In Numbers xxviii., xxix. the special offerings for each Jewish festival, with their number and accompanying meat-offerings and drink-offerings, are detailed at length. From this we learn, which of the feasts had reference only to Israel, and in which of them that which they prefigured concerned Gentiles as well. In Leviticus xxiii. Moses gives to Israel what may be called their ecclesiastical calendar, specifying the order in which the different festivals were to be kept, and the months and days appointed for their observance. So if we wished to understand the spirit in which any of the three great festivals were to be observed, we should turn to Deuteronomy xvi. to find out. If any inquired about the number and character of the different offerings, Numbers xxviii., xxix. would supply the answer; and Leviticus xxiii. would be consulted as the sacred calendar, informing all of the time and duration of each feast throughout the year. But to this arrangement there is one remarkable exception. Certain rites and sacrifices, connected both with the morrow after the paschal sabbath and with the feast of first-fruits, are mentioned in Leviticus, but are passed over in Numbers. Now why is this? Is the omission intentional, or is it accidental? It cannot be regarded as accidental, because, though some offerings specially appointed for the feast of first-fruits are enumerated in Numbers, where we should have looked for them, the new meat-offering, only described at length in Leviticus, is just mentioned in Numbers, though without a word being added in explanation of it. Evidently the sacred writer supposed his readers were acquainted with what had been written in Leviticus about it. He had not forgotten it, nor, from the way he introduces it, can we suppose that he was reminding his readers of it. He mentions that with which he and they were perfectly acquainted; but does not enter at length on the subject. The omission therefore of special instruction about it from that, (the forty-first section of the law according to the Jewish divisions of the Pentateuch) must have been intentional. Naturally we should have expected an account of it in Numbers, whereas we only learn about it in Leviticus. Had the Pentateuch been a mere human composition, would this arrangement have been met with? Had it been written by Moses simply with an eye to Israel, and what then concerned them, would he have thus arranged it? Surely not. But, as God's book, written under the immediate inspiration of the Holy Ghost, the subjects are treated of in God's order, and the wisdom of the divine plan becomes apparent. A glance at Leviticus xxiii. will make this plain.

And first, as to the new meat-offering presented to God at the feast of first-fruits. It was composed of two waveloaves, as they are called, baked with leaven; these two loaves typifying those from Jews and those from Gentiles, who as Christians are together presented to God, a kind of first-fruits of His creatures (James i. 18). It was not the oneness of the body of Christ that they portrayed, but that of which the body is composed, the two companies which together make up the one flock of John x. Baked with leaven, we learn that they represent saints still in their bodies on earth, and in whom the flesh exists. Made from the produce of the new harvest, we understand that they typify those who are before God as risen with Christ; for the close connection of Christians with Christ is set forth in the fact that the instruction about these two loaves is included in the same divine communication to Moses (Lev. xxiii. 9-22) which contains the ordinance concerning the wave-sheaf—the type of the Lord Jesus Himself as risen from the dead. Waved before the Lord, we see that the saints are claimed for God. Thus these loaves typify what Jews, as long as they remained Jews, never were—men on earth, yet risen with Christ. Typifying therefore those once Jews and those once Gentiles, brought to God on common ground, they speak of something really distinct from the earthly people, even the presentation to God of souls from Jews and Gentiles whom He can receive in connection with, and by virtue of, His acceptance of the sacrifice of the Lord Jesus Christ, and that whilst the *Lo-ammi* condition of Israel as a nation (Hosea i. 9) has not terminated.

But further. The feast of first-fruits was typical of the whole Christian era, which, commencing with the day of Pentecost, goes on to the rapture of which 1 Thess. iv. has apprised us. It prefigured therefore the time between the rejection of the Lord by the Jews, and their being gathered again to their land, to await His return previous to the commencement of millennial rest, of which the feast of Tabernacles is the type. As a feast of the Lord, it had its place in the sacred calendar; that is clear. But this chapter in Leviticus, besides serving as a sacred calendar for Israel, gives us in outline God's dealings with souls from Exodus to the eternal state; hence God's ways on earth, when Israel nationally are disowned, but the godly remnant saved, are fitly traced out in this portion of the Word. And had they been here omitted, there would have been, we can see, a gap in the prophetic outline of God's ways. But who, at the time when Moses wrote the book, could have discovered that? God alone, we may surely say, then knew it.

The Church then, we again see, was in the mind of God before it was presented to the eye of man; and as He divided to the nations their lot on earth with reference to His future dealings with Israel, so He guided Moses in the writing of His Word with reference to that subject of revelation, kept secret till revealed to Paul—the Church of the living God (Eph. iii. 3; Col. i. 25). And when the wave-loaves were brought to Him, and waved before Him, God looked on to that of which the Jews could never bear to hear—the presentation to Him of some, once Gentiles, on common and new ground with some formerly Jews. We may glory in this grace; yet let us remember that the thing waved was thereby publicly acknowledged as belonging to God. There is grace in being brought to God; there is responsibility in belonging to God.

CHAPTER VIII.

THE UNITY OF THE SPIRIT.

"ENDEAVORING to keep the unity of the Spirit in the bond of peace." Such is the word of exhortation addressed by the apostle Paul to Christians in the Epistle to the Ephesians (iv. 3). Then this of which he writes concerns Christians. As an exhortation, it acquaints us with God's desire for His children; but, at the same time, it indicates that we are in danger of not keeping the unity here mentioned.

Now the wisdom of this exhortation, and the positive need of it, has been abundantly manifested from that day to this. If we look at the state of Christendom, notably since the Reformation, but also before it, do we not learn from the pages of ecclesiastical history, how this not merely apostolic, but divine injunction has been sadly and systematically forgotten? Had it been remembered, and acted upon, one local assembly would never have been permitted to arrogate to itself control, by means of a local officer, over the actions and government of other assemblies, as the assembly at Rome has done, claiming for its bishop (a mere local officer, according to Scripture) jurisdiction over all the assemblies in Christendom. Had the apostolic injunction been practised, the question of precedence among what are called patriarchal sees would never have arisen. In the place of striving for pre-eminence, they would all have been jealous for the maintenance of the unity of the Spirit. Again, had the unity of the Spirit been understood, the rise of denominations in this country and elsewhere would have been checked, and the oneness of the body of Christ asserted, and upheld.

Unmindful of the existing unity of the Spirit, those in earlier days who had power and influence exerted it to organize the Church of God somewhat after the manner of the political administration of the Roman empire. Their acts prove how completely men had lost sight of the unity of the Spirit, and were substituting human organization for the authority of the divine Word, and the guidance of the Holy Ghost. What a monstrous assumption this was on the part of professing Christians! The sovereign action of the Holy Ghost was superseded, and His real presence ignored; and God's house, God's temple, received at the hands of His servants a constitution of man's devising! The Reformation afterwards took place. Many abuses were corrected, false doctrine on some important points was rejected, truth was disseminated in a way it had not been for ages; but the scripture teaching about the Church was not discerned, or if by any discerned, it was not acted upon. It did not apparently dawn on men's minds that God should direct as to the government of His house; for, whilst differing among themselves as to the form of church government, they all assumed that to man was left the power and authority of organizing the Church of God.

Brought up in one or other of those forms of man's devising, as most readers of these pages have been, and with the different schemes of church government in active operation around us, it becomes none of us, who through grace have been led to take a place outside of them, to point the finger at those who still adhere to, and uphold them. Rather be it our part, whilst keeping aloof from denominational ground, and helping others to see the solemn mistake of countenancing it, to be humbled at the recollection that we, however well intentioned, once helped on that which must in God's eyes savor of the grossest presumption; for it is presumption to suppose that God has left His house without any directions for its government. It is presumption for the servants of God practically to depose the Holy Ghost from His place in the Assembly, who has formed the unity which they are admonished to keep. What is here contended for, then, is not the liberty of any number of Christians to act as they will in the Church of God—a principle to which Scripture is wholly opposed; nor is it the liberty of private judgment which is insisted on, though we are individually responsible for our actions, and will be judged as individuals; but the positive duty of every Christian to submit in matters of church organization to the teaching of God's word, and to acknowledge the presence of the Holy Ghost in the Assembly, who divides to every man severally as He will (1 Cor. xii. 11).

Now what is it which Christians in general desiderate? Is it the manifestation of a oneness, the fruit of brotherhood? Is it the oneness of communion? Is it the oneness of the Spirit? All these are to be valued, and short of them all we should not any of us rest content. Would any settle down satisfied with manifesting the first? Then surely such have not entered into the mind of the Lord, as expressed to His Father on the night before His crucifixion. Would any remain unconcerned about the last? Then they would fall far short of God's desires for them.

Now the unity arising from brotherhood is nothing new. A Jew could speak of it, and Israel under David and Solomon must in measure have enjoyed it. The psalmist writes of it: "Behold, how good and how pleasant a thing it is for brethren to dwell together in unity!" (Psa. cxxxiii. 1.) All will echo this. The fruit of a tie formed by birth (for the psalmist writes of "brethren") reminds us that those here contemplated are members of one family, bound together by that bond which nothing can sever, and which no circumstances can really alter. One's brother must remain in that relation whatever may be the vicissitude of his affairs, or the character of his ways. The elder son in the parable was reminded that the prodigal was his brother (Luke xv. 32). The Thessalonian Christians were exhorted to count the saint their brother, even though he were walking disorderly, and not subject to the Word. Admonition under such circumstances would be needed. That was not to be spared; but the spiritual birth-tie existed, and was to be remembered. Of this they were reminded for their guidance in circumstances when there was the greatest danger of forgetting the link that God had formed between them (2 Thess. iii. 11-15).

Of course, the birth-tie of which the psalmist wrote was one after the order of nature. By-and-by Israel will fully enjoy what the writer describes, when the brotherhood between Israel and Judah, so long broken, shall be again owned, as Ezekiel, xxxvii. 15-22, has predicted. On the other hand, the tie of which Christians can speak is after a different order altogether (John i. 13). Still the statement of the psalmist will always hold good. It is good, it is pleasant, for brethren to dwell together in unity; yet this oneness, it is clear, may not always be manifested or enjoyed. It depends on the condition of those who, being brethren, ought to dwell together as such. As brethren, children of the same Father, Christians ought to dwell together in unity. Viewing their unity in this aspect, it is the family relationship, and what should flow from it, that rises up before the mind. Have we to speak of nothing else? The New Testament furnishes us with a decisive answer to the contrary. To that let us now turn.

The Lord Jesus Christ on the night before His crucifixion addressed His Father in the audience of His disciples. About to leave those whom He had drawn around Him during His ministry upon earth, He allowed the disciples to hear what was the nature of His desires on their behalf; and looking forward to the spread of the work which He had commenced, He embraced in the range of His petition every saint who should believe on Him through their word. "That they all may be one; as Thou, Father, art in Me, and I in Thee, that they also may be one in us: that the world may believe that Thou hast sent Me" (John xvii. 21). His prayer for oneness supposes both their need of it, and the danger there might be of their not enjoying it. He does not ask that the oneness of brotherhood should be formed; that takes place by birth. He asks that the oneness of communion should exist and be seen, explaining what He means by the illustration He adduces, "As Thou, Father, art in Me, and I in Thee." The Father in the Son, and the Son in the Father, there must be between these two perfect communion. No thoughts, no desires, has the Son which are opposed to the Father; no thoughts has the Father which are not in full accord with the wishes of the Son. This oneness of communion He desired for His people. They would in this manner be one, and the world would believe that the Father had sent the Son. Of this character of oneness Paul writes to the Corinthians (1 Cor. i. 10), and presses earnestly on the Philippians (ii. 3 ; iv. 2.)

Now the continuance of this oneness depends on the condition of the saints. Communion one with another, as we but too well know, may be easily interrupted and broken. The nature capable of enjoying it, Christians possess; but they have also a nature strongly opposed to it. Hence the oneness the Lord prayed for depends on the state of the saints. His wish about it is plain; the result of it as regards the world He also declares. The world could take cognizance of it, and be affected by it. One in the Father and in the Son, there would be amongst God's people real and perfect communion.

There is, however, a third oneness of which the Word treats, and treats in a different way. It did not form the subject of the Lord's petitions on the night before His cross. It did not then exist; for it had not been formed, and could not be formed, till the Lord had gone on high. It does, however, exist now; because the Holy Ghost has made it, by baptizing all believers into one body. It is of this Paul wrote, when he exhorted believers to endeavor to keep the unity of the Spirit in the bond of peace.

In the Gospel, where the Lord explains His meaning, He speaks of the Father and of Himself. In the Epistle, where the unity of which the apostle writes is to be defined, it is called the unity of the Spirit. Of course it is only by the Holy Ghost acting in us that we can manifest oneness of communion. To illustrate it, however, we are reminded of the Father and the Son, between whom there was, there is, perfect, uninterrupted communion; for the Father is in the Son, and the Son is in the Father. By being one in the Father and in the Son, the saints would manifest a oneness of the same character. In Ephesians, on the other hand, there is nothing of all this. There is a unity mentioned as existing, which they are exhorted to keep. For oneness of communion to be manifested and maintained, prayer was made by the Lord on our behalf. When the keeping the unity of the Spirit is the subject in hand, exhortation, not prayer, is immediately called forth.

Now this of which Paul writes is not oneness of spirit. Often it may have been mistaken for that. To view the exhortation in that light is really to confound what the Lord prayed for with that of which the apostle here writes. How could oneness of spirit be maintained except in the bond of peace? The words of the apostle, however, suppose there may be a difficulty in thus keeping it; for he writes, "Endeavoring" to keep it "in the bond of peace." One body formed by one Spirit existed, and all true believers belonged to it. They did not themselves originate the unity, nor could they break it; but they were to keep it in the bond of peace. Its formation, its continuance, are both independent of the spiritual condition of God's saints, though none but real saints can form part of it. It concerns them, then, very closely, for they are the body of Christ, and God's habitation in the Spirit.

Into the closest of associations believers are therefore now brought. One new man in Christ, the body of Christ, God's habitation now in the Spirit, stones too of the temple of God which is in process of erection—these are the terms used by the Holy Ghost of those, once dead in trespasses and sins, who have been quickened together with Christ, raised up together, and made to sit together in heavenly places in Christ. As new creatures in Christ, they are brought into this unity; whilst the old man, the flesh, is still within them. Hence exhortations are added that they should "walk worthy of the vocation wherewith they are called, with all lowliness and meekness, with long-suffering, forbearing one another in love; endeavoring to keep the unity of the Spirit in the bond of peace." For a position of such close relationship calls for much consideration and activity of love one towards another. The fact that we are exhorted, proves we may fail in acting aright. The burden of the exhortation indicates what should characterize each one of us. Care, thoughtfulness, forbearance, love, should be manifested; but at the same time the saints are never to forget that unity which the Holy Ghost has formed; nor is the keeping of it to be sacrificed to the maintenance of friendliness, or what is miscalled love; for the love of God will not be manifested unless we keep His commandments (1 John v. 3). In this way, then, are we to endeavor to keep it.

Now the term, the unity of the Spirit, points to that with which He is in a special manner connected, even the body which He has formed, according to 1 Cor. xii. 13. If, then, we are to keep it, the common idea of agreeing to differ on matters of church organization must evidently be abandoned. Nor that only; for the exhortation leaves us no choice, no alternative, but to own, and, as far as in us lies, to keep the unity of the Spirit in the bond of peace. For since the component parts of that unity are those in whom the flesh still exists, the reminder of the uniting bond of peace is not without significance and use. And since this unity exists, Christians should learn about it; for how can we endeavor to keep that which we do not know exists?

But is this what all are desirous of? It is no secret that there is the consciousness in many a heart that Christians are not practically united as they might be, and should be. One they are before God, members of the one body, being united by the Holy Ghost to the one Head, baptized by Him into one body. All ideas, then, of merely acknowledging that we are one, without seeking practically to own it in God's appointed way, are clearly not in harmony with God's will or God's word. How, then, shall we correct what is wrong? By forming some new union? By maintaining denominational ground? Clearly neither of these expedients is right. We are to keep what the Holy Ghost has formed, and endeavor to do it in the bond of peace. To form a church, or to organize a union, is virtually to fly in the face of God's injunctions for His people. To attempt to make something for the uniting together of God's saints is virtually to disown what the Spirit has already done. To continue on denominational ground, when once we see it to be wrong, is openly to ignore what has been formed, and to hinder ourselves and others from keeping the unity of the Spirit in the bond of peace.

CHAPTER IX.

THE MINISTRY OF THE WORD.

HAVING viewed the Church in its relation to God, to the Lord Jesus Christ, and to the Holy Ghost, and having also seen how the Body is formed, we would next direct the reader's attention to the way in which the work of God is carried on during this dispensation.

The Assembly of the living God is the pillar and ground of the truth (1 Tim. iii. 15). Outside of it God's truth has no resting-place on earth. In it only can be found the truth of which that passage speaks. And it is only by the ministry of the Word, in some form or other, that the work of God upon earth can make progress, and the number of His children be increased. Now when God was dealing with His chosen people Israel, He raised up prophets to speak to their consciences, and to acquaint them with the purposes of His heart. For the most part, they exclusively addressed themselves to the nation of Israel, having for their audience those who were of the seed of Jacob. In so far as their ministry took effect on souls, its then present purpose was accomplished. But all the labors of the prophets, however successful they might have been, could not have increased the number of God's earthly people, inasmuch as they had their place in Israel by virtue of their natural birth. Their service was to act upon that people who were in a place of outward relationship to God.

With the rejection by the Jews of the testimony of the

THE MINISTRY OF THE WORD.

Lord, a new work commenced, viz., the forming of a company upon earth in true relationship to God as His children, and His people. Into this family none could find an entrance on the ground of earthly ties, or by the effort of human will. In it relationship by *new* birth was acknowledged, but blood-relationship was unknown. To become children of God souls must be born of God (Jno. i. 12, 13). Hence this mighty change could only be effected by the will of God. Of God's will in the matter James writes (i. 18); of the instrumentality of the Word that same apostle, in common with Peter (1 Peter i. 23), makes distinct mention. And it seems fitting that these two among the apostles, whose work lay especially amongst God's ancient people, should insist on the truth of a new birth, when writing to those who had been regarded as children of the Kingdom on the ground of their Abrahamic descent.

In the synagogue service, after the reading of the law and of the prophets, there was room for exhortation (Acts xiii. 15) to press home on the hearts of those present the lessons to be deduced from the Scriptures. But, it became evident, more than this was required if the number of God's children could only be increased by the action of the divine Word upon the soul, and if some from amongst Gentiles were to become children in common with some from amongst Jews. A ministry, therefore, which could first convert, and then build up the converts, was called for.

Now this God provided, and the Lord, in the parable of the sower, indicated. For God was not about any longer to seek fruit from those who were His people on the ground of their descent from Abraham; He was henceforth going to beget children by water and the Spirit, who should be able to be fruitful for Him. Not that the exercise of quickening power by the Word was anything new in itself in the ways of God, for every saint, from Abel downward, had been born of God; but those whom He would now own as really His people would only be such as were in truth His children. Hence God commenced to work afresh, and the Lord appeared in the character of the sower. Now a field, till sown, can manifestly produce no good crop. The ground may have been all prepared for the seed, but unless the seed is sown no good results can be expected. To sow, then, indicates the commencement of a work, and the place of the parable of the sower in the three synoptic Gospels agrees with this.

In Matthew, who gives us dispensational teaching, the parable only comes in when the ground has been cleared by the Lord's judgment of the cities where He had worked (xi.), and of the nation amongst whom He was laboring (xii.). Then, declaring the character of the relationship to Himself which He would henceforth acknowledge, even that of the new birth, evidenced by the individual doing the will of His Father who is in the heavens, He left the house, and sat by the seaside, and there, with multitudes collected from various parts of the land (Luke viii. 4), He gave utterance to the parable of the sower; His very action and place of teaching both harmonizing with the work which God was commencing. In Mark the parable is given us in the fourth chapter of his Gospel, as forming part, and the commencing part, of the Lord's instruction to His disciples ere He sent them forth to preach. For the reader may observe that, though chosen in chap. iii. 14–19, they are not sent forth to preach till chap. vi. 7; the intervening part of the Gospel being occupied with instructing them in what God was doing, in order to fit them to do their work for God, and for the Lord. In Luke the same parable appears (chap. viii.), in common with several things which are characteristic features of the Kingdom.

With this ministry of the Lord, then, a fresh beginning was made. He sowed the word of the Kingdom, the word of God, and thus taught us how the Kingdom, during His rejection, can be really advanced. Going about from town to town, and from village to village, He preached and showed the glad tidings of the Kingdom of God (Luke viii. 1). In this He was followed by the twelve, when sent forth by Him on their special mission to Israel (Luke ix. 2, 6). After He rose, the field of labor became enlarged, reaching even to the utmost bounds of the earth; so that wherever there should be a soul to hear and a messenger to carry the Word, there was a sphere in which God's servant could work in accordance with the divine mind.

The effects of the sower's labors the parable describes. The seed was pure; it was the word of God. Of its germinating power there could be no doubt; for that Word liveth and abideth (1 Peter i. 23); so the only hindrance to a full crop, wherever it fell, would arise from the condition of the ground; in other words, the man's heart to whom it might come. Men might think of blaming the Word for the apparent failure of the work. Against such thoughts the Lord would warn us, and the continued going on of God's work should guard us. For as the seed is the word of God (Luke viii. 11), the word of the Kingdom, as Matthew xiii. 19 describes it, the lack of full results must evidently arise from other causes than the character of the Word; and to these the parable directs us. In saying this, however, it must be borne in mind that we are only treating of the seed, and not of any instrument by whom in these days the seed may be scattered. Through admixture of rubbish with the seed, from a want of right apprehension as to what the seed is, much labor may be in vain, and efforts be found to be fruitless. But where the real seed is sown, the want of a crop will not arise from lack of its germinating power. It is the living word of God. We do well to remember this, that all who preach or teach may make sure that it is the word of God they are using, and count on its sufficiency, as applied by the Holy Ghost, to effect a divine work in the hearts and consciences of men.

The causes which hinder a fruitful crop are three. First, some men do not desire the Word, in which case the devil takes it away. Secondly, the conscience has not been reached by the Word, so the apparent work is but ephemeral, and dies away. Thirdly, the attraction of, or occupation with, surrounding things, chokes the Word, and it becomes unfruitful. For those only are fruitful who hear the Word, understand it (Matt. xiii. 23), receive it (Mark iv. 20), and keep it (Luke viii. 15). Two important things, then, are manifested by this way of working: the first is the condition of man's heart by nature; and the second is the positive need for God to work in it, if fruit, which He can acknowledge as such, is to be produced at all. The wisdom, too, of this way of working becomes apparent. For what penal restrictions could not accomplish (Gen. viii. 21), nor law effect, God does by His Word, winning souls to Himself, and making them willing servants of Christ. And Satan, by taking away the seed sown, where he can, or by imitating God's method of working and becoming a sower himself, as the parable of the tares and the wheat teaches us, attests the

THE MINISTRY OF THE WORD.   89

wisdom of God in thus working by His Word. For he who imitates the work of another confesses that he has nothing better to suggest, and knows no plan more effectual to work by. But here a distinction should be noted. In the parable of the sower it is the commencement of a fresh work to which attention is directed, and God's word is the seed which acts on men, and alone can make them fruitful. It is the sowing that we there read of. In the parable of the tares, on the other hand, a parable of the Kingdom of the heavens, which the former parable is not, we have presented the results evident to the outward eyes of the sower's labors. So persons are mentioned as being in the field. It is the growing crop to which attention is directed, and the efforts of the enemy to counteract God's work. For the explanation given us of the parable tells us that the children of the Kingdom are the fruit of the good seed, and the children of the wicked one are the fruit of the enemy's work. Till the Lord came, the Jews looked on themselves as the sons of the Kingdom (Matt. viii. 12). In this parable we are taught who such really are (xiii. 38); for publicans and harlots justified God by entering into the Kingdom through really receiving the seed, the word of God, whilst Pharisees, scribes, the self-righteous and the indifferent shut themselves out of it.

After the Lord rose, the full extent of the field in which His people were to work by the instrumentality of the Word was clearly defined. Repentance and remission of sins was to be preached among all nations, beginning at Jerusalem (Luke xxiv. 47), and unto the uttermost part of the earth were the disciples to be witnesses to Christ (Acts i. 8); but first they must be endued with power from on high by the coming on them of the Holy Ghost.

But could the preaching of the word of God really deal in power with hearts? Peter's address on the day of Pentecost proved what it could do, as three thousand of his hearers were pricked to the heart by his words, and, implicitly obeying his directions, were numbered henceforth as disciples in truth of the despised and crucified Nazarene.

In the very town, then, where the Lord had been so lately crucified, the work commenced of adding together such as should be saved (Acts ii. 47); and this was effected by the instrumentality of the Word. The movement did not originate in some obscure village of Galilee, and, when it could boast of numbers, display itself to the world; but just six weeks after the crucifixion of the Lord, and in the very centre of Judaism, in the metropolitan city, Jerusalem, under the shadow, as it were, of the temple, the words of life were spoken which bowed hearts to confess the Crucified One as their Saviour and their Lord. The work thus commenced, nothing could stop. Peter and John were arrested, and put in ward; but many who heard their word believed, and the number of the men now swelled to about five thousand souls (Acts iv. 4). At a little later date, when the opposition of the Sanhedrin became more marked, the sacred historian acquaints us with the onward march of the work. "The word of God increased; and the number of the disciples multiplied in Jerusalem greatly; and a great company of the priests were obedient to the faith" (vi. 7). Like the waters of Ezekiel (xlvii.), each time the stream is, as it were, measured, it is only to tell of its expansion in breadth, as well as of its ceaseless flow. And resembling that river in another character, the movement, as it spread over the land of Israel, and reached even to Gentiles, disseminated life to all who profited by it.

In Samaria, by the preaching of Philip, souls were evangelized, and Simon Magus found himself eclipsed (Acts viii.). The preaching of Christ had more effect, he saw, than his sorceries and bewitchments. Amongst the Gentiles the effects were the same. The sorcerer Bar-jesus was unable to turn away Sergius Paulus from the faith (xiii. 6–12). Idolaters turned from idols to God (1 Thess. i. 9), and from such sounded out the word of the Lord; for the gospel had come to them "in power, and in the Holy Ghost, and in much assurance." Men saw and acknowledged a force at work to which Gentiles had hitherto been strangers. God was working by His Word in the power of the Holy Ghost. Ignorant heathen (Acts xiv. 21; xvi. 34) and educated heathen alike were reached by the Word. In Corinth, the seat of licentiousness; in Ephesus, a great centre of idolatry; in Rome, the metropolis of the empire, the gospel made its way. Magical books were burnt by their owners at Ephesus; and in the very household of the emperor Nero the Lord Jesus had some of His sheep (Phil. iv. 22). Thus, from high and low, rich and poor, masters and slaves, souls were numbered amongst the disciples of Christ. For the word of God had reached them, and they had received it as His Word, which effectually works in those that believe. Nor was it that one like Paul, by the force of his ardor, drew men along with him; for where he had not labored the work spread, and the Word ministered wrought with like power. Of this the Colossians are an example (Col. i. 6–8). For as at Rome, so at Colosse, the assembly there existing was not formed by the labors of the apostle.

If such were some of the results of the ministry of the Word, what was the subject of it? It was Christ. Philip preached Christ (Acts viii. 5). His death, His resurrection, His ascension, were freely proclaimed (Acts ii. 23-34; iv. 33; 1 Cor. xv. 3-8), and forgiveness and justification from all things formed part of the glad tidings (Acts x. 43; xiii. 38, 39). Truth, too, about His person was set forth, that He is the Son of God (Acts ix. 20; Rom. i. 1-4). As the message from God to men, it was called the gospel, or glad tidings of God (Rom. i. 1; 1 Thess. ii. 2). As the truth about the Lord Jesus was its subject, it was called the gospel of the Christ (Rom. xv. 19; Phil. i. 27). And as it set forth God's ways with men in grace, it was called the gospel of the grace of God (Acts xx. 24). Of the power of this message, Paul, who had often carried it about, bears testimony. He was not ashamed of the gospel, "for it is the power of God unto salvation to every one that believeth; to the Jew first, and also to the Greek" (Rom. i. 16); and from Jerusalem round about unto Illyricum he had fully preached the gospel of the Christ (xv. 19). In doing this he had moved among men of different minds, and nations characterized by different habits. Orientals had heard from his lips the glad tidings of salvation. Europeans too had listened to it, and received it. Led about by God in triumph in Christ, he carried from place to place the testimony with which he had been intrusted. He did not alter the message to suit the temper of his hearers; for Christ crucified, whom he preached, was both the wisdom of God and the power of God to those who were called, whether from Jews or Greeks (1 Cor. i. 24). What confidence he manifested in the power and suitability of the divine Word to meet all classes and conditions of men! But besides the preaching of the gospel of the grace of God, the Kingdom also was preached, and everywhere there was insisted on "repentance toward God, and faith toward our Lord Jesus Christ" (Acts xx. 20–25).

But not only did ministering brethren preach, they also taught. Of Philip, the evangelist, we only read that he preached (Acts viii. 5, 12, 35, 40). Of Barnabas we learn that he could exhort* (Acts xi. 23); and when he brought Saul to Antioch, teaching went on in that assembly (ver. 26), gathered out by the preaching of those who went there upon the persecution that arose about Stephen (vers. 19–21). Thus by the exercise of different gifts the work was carried on. Some, as Philip, it would seem, may have been only evangelists; others, as Judas and Silas, may have been well known for their abilities as prophets to exhort (Acts xv. 32); others again, as Barnabas, and preeminently Paul, were gifted to teach, and to preach, and to press home on the conscience the word of God. But each in their measure, and as gifted by the Spirit, and being themselves gifts from the ascended Christ, helped on God's work on earth. And the Word was the weapon relied on, and used. They wanted no other; they turned to no other to deal with the conscience, and bow the heart. Moreover, they knew the character of that weapon, and its temper too; for what they relied on to bring every thought to the obedience of Christ was "the sword of the Spirit"—God's own word (Eph. vi. 17).

The different gifts of ministry, and the distinct lines of ministry, are marked in the Word. There was preaching and teaching, as there were evangelists, pastors, and teachers. At Jerusalem they ceased not to teach and to

---

* It was perhaps from his possession of this gift of exhorting that the apostles surnamed him Barnabas, interpreted in Greek *Son of exhortation, or consolation* (Acts iv. 36).

preach that Jesus was the Christ (Acts v. 42). At Antioch Paul and Barnabas continued teaching and preaching the word of the Lord (xv. 35). At Ephesus (xx.), at Corinth (xviii. 11; 1 Cor. i.), at Rome (xxviii. 31), and elsewhere (Col. i. 23-28), Paul continued to do both; for whilst by evangelizing the Assembly is increased, there are things which form the subject of teaching, and not of preaching. Hence, if the work of God is to progress healthily, both teaching and preaching are requisite. Where simple evangelizing is all that is sought after, the saints will not be fully instructed in the truth; where that is depreciated or neglected, interest in the spread of God's work is in danger of flagging.

CHAPTER X.

PRAYER AND PRAYER MEETINGS.

BY the ministry of the Word souls receive life, light, and understanding. As recipients of life there are desires formed within them which need an outgate, either by prayer or by worship. By the former, dependence upon God is confessed and expressed; by the latter, relief is afforded to the heart, in the enjoyment of God's love, through the pouring itself out before Him. If the sense of need is uppermost within us, whether for ourselves, for others, or for the work of God upon earth, prayer is the way in which it expresses itself. If it be the exceeding riches of God's grace upon which the soul is dwelling, worship will be found to give it proper and satisfying relief. Thus graciously does God afford His people an outlet for their hearts, His ear being open to hear whatever they have to say to Him. To a consideration of prayer let us now address ourselves.

Man's proper place is one of dependence upon God, and this the Lord, though God as well as man, frequently manifested in His own life on earth. He prayed; He spent a whole night in prayer; He prayed earnestly; He prayed in secret; He prayed openly. In the wilderness, on the mount, on Jordan's brink, and in the garden of. Gethsemane, the Lord Jesus Christ poured out His soul in prayer to God.

Prayer too, public and private, characterized the early Christians. Of the first converts we read: "They continued stedfastly in the apostles' doctrine and fellowship, and in breaking of bread, and in prayers" (Acts ii. 42). Their enjoyment of the grace of God did not lead to forgetfulness of their dependence upon God; nor in the hour of God's interposition on their behalf did they fail to remember how all their resources were in Him. For when Peter and John, who had been taken before the council, were restored to their own company, the hostility of the ecclesiastical rulers to the spread of the truth having now become manifest, the whole company, to whom the two apostles reported all that the chief priests and rulers had said to them, lifted up their voice with one accord to God for the continued successful prosecution of the work (Acts iv. 24). Again, when Peter was in prison, arrested by the political power which at that time had sway at Jerusalem, and his martyrdom was determined upon for the morrow, fervent prayer was made on his behalf, and a prayer meeting was held for that purpose in the house of Mary the mother of John, surnamed Mark (Acts xii.). And that meeting had not broken up, though it was past the hour of midnight, when Peter in person announced to them how their prayer had been heard, and his release had been effected. Nor was it only in Jerusalem that meetings for prayer were held; for when the Holy Ghost had marked out Barnabas and Paul at Antioch for the work to which He had called them, prophets and teachers there assembled laid their hands on them, after fasting and prayer, recommending them to the grace of God for the work they had been called on to undertake (Acts xiii. 3; xiv. 26). On another occasion, at Tyre, when Paul was on his way to Jerusalem for his last visit there of which we have any record, the whole assembly, including the wives and children, knelt down in prayer outside the city, on the sea-shore, with those of

Paul's company (Acts xxi. 5). A refreshment, doubtless, this must have been to the apostle's heart—a service, too, well-pleasing to God.

Besides these instances of common prayer, in which the whole company took part, we learn from Scripture how repeatedly saints were wont to resort to it. The twelve, when exercising their apostolic powers in appointing the seven deacons, engaged in prayer before they laid their hands upon them (Acts vi. 6). Similarly, Paul and Barnabas, when appointing elders in every city, prayed with fasting, and commended them to the Lord, on whom they had believed (Acts xiv. 23). Peter and John, in Samaria, prayed that the converts might receive the Holy Ghost previous to the laying on of their hands to bestow it (Acts viii. 15). Peter, too, when raising up Dorcas from the dead (Acts ix. 40), and Paul, when about to heal the father of Publius (Acts xxviii. 8), alike confessed their entire dependence upon God for the exercise of such powers on man's behalf. Of Stephen we read that his latest utterance was one of intercession for his murderers (Acts vii. 60). Of Paul we learn that, though the character of his future work was told him at his conversion ere he rose from the ground (Acts xxvi. 17, 18),* yet it was when engaged in prayer in the temple at Jerusalem, that he received his directions to depart to the Gentiles (Acts xxii. 17, 18). In the house which was left desolate to the Jews, for the presence of the Lord was not there, the divine command to depart to the Gentiles was communicated directly to the vessel fitted for the service. On another occasion, in a place and under circumstances very different from the last, Paul and Silas, in the prison at Philippi, with their feet made fast in the

---

* "Now" in verse 17 is ommited in all uncial MSS.

stocks, at midnight prayed, and sang praises to God. Their bodies were subjected to the power and malice of man. Their spirits were free, and unfettered. They prayed, and they sang praises to God (Acts xvi. 25), and an answer came. God acted in power and in grace. An earthquake shook the prison, opened its doors, and set the prisoners free; and the word of God, by Paul and Silas, converted the jailer and his household. Again, at Miletus, the apostle did not bring to a close his farewell interview with the Ephesian elders, until he had prayed with them (Acts xx.). How prayer characterized him his epistles demonstrate (Rom. i. 9, 10; Eph. i. 16; iii. 14; Phil. i. 4; Col. i. 3; 1 Thess. i. 2; 2 Tim. i. 3; Phile. 4). How he valued the prayers of others, and counted on them, his epistles also teach us (Rom. xv. 30; Eph. vi. 18,19; Phil. i. 7; * Col. iv. 3; 1 Thess. v. 25; 2 Thess. iii. 1; Phile. 22; Heb. xiii. 18). But he seems not to have asked the prayers of any who were walking in ways that he had to reprove. To the Galatians he made no request for their fellowship with him in prayer, though we cannot doubt from the tone of his letter that he prayed for them (Gal. iv. 19). Nor did he solicit the prayers of the Corinthians till Titus had assured him of their godly sorrow. A silence of this kind on the part of the apostle has surely a voice for us. To ask for the prayers of others should never be a matter of form on our part.

Prayer for one's self (James v. 13); prayer for others, for saints (Eph. vi. 18), and for all men (1 Tim. ii. 1); prayer too for the work of God upon earth (Col. iv. 3, 4) —with such requests are we permitted, and exhorted, to

---

*" Because ye have me in your heart," not "because I have you in my heart," is what the apostle really expressed.

approach God. Nor is this anything new; for saints in Old Testament times addressed Him, and in accordance with the revelation of their day drew nigh to God as the Almighty (Job viii. 5), or as Jehovah God of Israel (1 Kings viii. 23), who dwelleth between the cherubim (2 Kings xix. 15). As seated on His earthly throne, Israel adressed to Him their supplications. Christians, however, are privileged to call on God as their Father who is in the heavens, and to pray likewise to the Lord Jesus Christ (2 Cor. xii. 8); but nowhere are they authorized in Scripture to pray to the Holy Ghost. Praying *in* the Holy Ghost (Jude 20; Eph. vi. 18) is what Christians are exhorted to do; but never are they told to pray *to* Him. Praying in the Holy Ghost we shall express the desires which the Spirit of God has formed in our hearts, and as the Spirit would lead us to present them; and, as having access to the heavenly sanctuary, we pray to Him who is in the heavens. Prayer then should ever be in accordance with the revelation vouchsafed to God's saints. What was suited to Solomon and Hezekiah would not be fitting for us. We should not address God as the God of Israel, nor speak to Him as dwelling between the cherubim. Similarly, since the Holy Ghost is with us, making intercession too for us according to God (Rom. viii. 27), and with the Bride asks the Lord Jesus to come (Rev. xxii. 17), addresses to Him, whether invoking His presence on earth, or asking Him to help us, receive no countenance from the divine Word, and indicate a lack of spiritual understanding in those who do so.

Prayer to God as the Father was first taught by the Son, who reveals Him (Matt. xi. 27). Taught by Him about the Father, the disciples asked the Lord how they were to pray; for clearly the old forms of prayer did not meet the position into which they were brought by this revelation on the part of the Son. To their desire He responded, and gave them what is commonly called the Lord's Prayer (Matt. vi. 9-13),—without the doxology, which does not form part of the true text. Now this act on the Lord's part is full of instruction for us. John the Baptist, who had ministered truth for his day, taught his disciples how to pray. The Lord Jesus, who revealed the Father, taught also His disciples (some of whom certainly had been disciples of John) how *they* were to pray. The old Jewish forms of prayer clearly no longer suited the disciples of Christ. The prayer, or prayers, John taught his disciples ceased to be the proper expression of their heart, when they had learnt from the Son about the Father. It is plain, then, that prayer should always be in harmony with, and based upon, the revelation of God which has been vouchsafed us. Souls in those days felt that. The Lord then endorsed the thought as correct, and afterwards abundantly confirmed it; for just before His departure, on the night previous to His crucifixion, unasked by the eleven, He discoursed in a marked way on this important subject. Of the power of prayer, when offered up in faith, He had taught them only a few days before (Matt. xxi. 21, 22; Mark xi. 22-24). Now, in the immediate prospect of His departure, He teaches them a good deal more. He was about to leave them to go the Father, henceforth to be hidden from their sight. They should, however, have a clear proof that He was where He had told them that He was going; for they should do greater works than He had done, and whatsoever they should ask in His name, that He would do, **that the Father might be glorified in the Son, adding, "If** ye shall ask anything in My name, I will do it" (John xiv. 12–14). The world, the Jews, might taunt them with trusting to a crucified man; but as answers came to prayers offered up in His name, they would have abundant proof, both that He was with the Father, accepted on high, though rejected on earth, and also that He was caring for His own.

Now here for the first time do we read of prayer to be offered up in His name. When He gave His disciples the prayer of Matt. vi. He did not tell them to present their petitions in His name; and in John xvi. 24 we distinctly learn from His own lips that this was something quite new. "Hitherto," He said, "have ye asked nothing in My name: ask, and ye shall receive, that your joy may be full." The prayer of Matt. vi. was prayer to the Father, the pouring out of the heart to God from one that knew himself to be His child; but, till the atonement by the blood of Christ was accomplished, prayer in His name was unknown. As soon as that was effected, and known by those who believed on Him, prayer was to be offered up in His name. His name would henceforth have a meaning for them as well as for God; for it expresses all that He is in the eyes of God the Father. The answer would come from God; but the Son it would be who would fulfil the desires of their hearts. "I will do it" assured them of this, and of His unabated interest in all that concerned them.

But further, since unlimited power was at His command to do whatsoever they asked, He proceeded to tell them on what conditions all their requests would be granted. "If ye abide in Me, and My words abide in you, ye shall ask what ye will, and it shall be done unto you" (John xv. 7). Conforming to these conditions—

for they are conditions—they could reckon on asking the right things, and could be sure of receiving an answer. For, if abiding in Christ, and His words abiding in them, they would be in the current of God's thoughts, and hence their desires would be quite in conformity with His mind. Further, He added, "Ye have not chosen Me, but I have chosen you, and ordained you, that ye should go and bring forth fruit and that your fruit should remain; that whatsoever ye shall ask of the Father in My name, He may give it you" (John xv. 16). Here He again lays down conditions, and mentions the name of the One to whom they were to address themselves, which as yet in this discourse He had not stated. And now one more point had to be noticed, ere His instructions on the subject of prayer were complete; viz., the time from whence they might begin thus to pray. "At that day," *i. e.*, after His resurrection, "ye shall ask in My name; and I say not unto you, that I will pray the Father for you: for the Father Himself loveth you, because ye have loved Me, and have believed that I came out from God" (John xvi. 26, 27). Familiar, personal intercourse with the Lord as man upon the earth would cease; for He would be no longer present with them in the manner that He had been. They would therefore in that day ask nothing of Him; but whatsoever they should ask the Father in His name, the Father would give them (John xvi. 23). So direct was to be their intercourse with the Father, and such a valid plea would they be able always to urge before Him.

Four distinct points then are taken up by the Lord in these three chapters of John's Gospel. 1st. In whose name we are to pray (xiv.); 2nd., conditions on which, if fulfilled, we can be sure of answers to our requests;

3rd., the One to whom we can pray (xv.); and, 4th., the time when the Lord's instructions were first to be acted on (xvi.). Whilst, then, we can always present our requests to God the Father, who is never weary of harkening to the cry of His children, and whilst we have a plea on which to base our petitions—a plea the full value of which is known, not to us, but to Him to whom we pray—there are, we must ever remember, conditions laid down, conforming to which we can reckon upon an answer to our prayers; viz., faith, as set forth in Matt. xxi., and the conditions stated in the Gospel by John. A remembrance of these will surely check rash and inconsiderate petitions. Can I link the name of Christ with the prayer I am presenting to the Father? Have I the mind of God as to that which I am solicitous to get? Can I profer my requests in faith?

These remarks apply to prayer in general, both private and public. Liberty to resort to the former is freely given us in the Epistles (Rom. xii. 12; Eph. vi. 18; Phil. iv. 6; Col. iv. 2; 1 Thess. v. 17; 1 Pet. iv. 7). Instructions about the latter are set forth in 1 Tim. ii. Of common prayer the Lord also has made mention in Matt. xviii. 19, 20, assuring His disciples that if only two should agree touching anything they might ask, it should be done for them of His Father who is in the heavens; for where two or three are gathered together unto His name, there is He in the midst of them. On His presence then we can reckon, if the condition laid down is complied with —gathered unto His name; for of that His people need never be deprived, however small their number, though they are upon earth and He is in heaven.

Now this supposes a meeting for prayer, directions for which Timothy received from Paul. For, what the order of such a meeting should be, it is not left to man to devise. How various in that case the arrangements would surely be! God, however, has given us by the apostle His regulations in connection with it. And such were needed: for since Christianity restores woman to her proper place in connection with man, which among the heathen was lost, and Judaism did not teach (Matt. xix. 8), though she is still subject to God's governmental dealings, the consequence of the fall; and since too the saints were taught that in Christ there is neither male nor female (Gal. iii. 28), there was a danger—and the state of matters shows it had already risen—lest they should confound the condition in Christ with the relative position of the sexes in the Assembly. In Christ we are all one; in the Assembly we are not. The grace shown to us in Christ does not override God's order in creation. This the Corinthians had to be taught (1 Cor. xi. 1–9), and of this Timothy is reminded.

Looking at that chapter, we can form a very good idea of what a prayer meeting must have been in apostolic times, if all gathered together were in subjection to the teaching of the Word. Composed of persons of both sexes, the men only opened their mouths in prayer, any one of whom, however, was free, if guided by the Spirit, to lead the whole company in their devotions. "For I will," wrote the apostle, "that the men pray everywhere." Both the men and the women were indwelt by the Holy Ghost; for He then, and now, dwells in every true believer. The fact, then, of having received the Holy Ghost did not make such an one fit to lead others in prayer. All were one in Christ; but God's order in the Assembly was to be observed, although, as it would seem, the separation of the sexes, carried out in the synagogue, was not maintained in the Christian assembly. Might then any man, because of his sex, make himself the mouthpiece of the company in their devotions? Assuming that he was otherwise able to do it, he would nevertheless, on any occasion, have been disqualified, if he could not lift up holy (or pious) hands without wrath and reasoning. What creatures then they were in themselves in the assembly at Ephesus, since such a caution was required! "Just like me," however, every one, who knows something of his evil nature, must surely acknowledge. What grace then to allow such to approach the throne of grace on behalf of themselves, and as the mouthpieces of the assembly of God!

If we had been present at such a meeting, we should have found the women, who were obedient to the apostolic injunctions, adorned in seemly guise, with modesty and discretion; and, instead of setting off their persons by jewels or costly array, had we watched their general behaviour, followed them to their homes, and spent a day in their company, we should have seen them adorned with ornaments of great value indeed, such as become women professing godliness, even with good works. Further, whilst in the assembly they would all have been silent (1 Cor. xiv. 34); elsewhere we should have found them, surely, learning in quietness, not teaching nor usurping authority over the men; but being in quietness, remembering both woman's place in creation, as evidenced by the fact that Adam was first formed, then Eve, and the fatal consequences of her intercourse in the garden with the serpent. The woman was deceived; the man was not. Adam harkened to the voice of his wife. and she proved her unfitness to take the lead. "Nevertheless," adds the apostle, "she shall be preserved in child-bearing, if they continue in faith and charity and holiness with sobriety." Inasmuch as the head of the woman is the man, her preservation in child-bearing is connected governmentally as much with the husband's behavior as with her own.

Having glanced at the orderly arrangement of a prayer meeting, we may in conclusion inquire, What would have been the character of their prayers. Very comprehensive they might be, and very free. Bound by no written or pre-arranged form, they could freely make use of all the different kinds of prayer with which we are acquainted. Supplications, prayers, intercession and giving of thanks, they were free to present before the throne of grace. Addressing the High and Holy One with all the reverence and solemnity that befits a creature addressing its God, they could nevertheless speak to Him in all the confidence of children, being free to express every desire, and to lay before Him all the wants and wishes of the assembly. The grace this speaks of is great. God would be entreated of them. He would harken to their prayers. He would let them hold free, personal intercourse with Him; for such $\mathit{\unicode{x1F10}}\nu\tau\varepsilon\upsilon\xi\iota\varsigma$,* translated intercession, seems to imply. And to thanksgivings also they were free to give utterance on such occasions. For if mindful of the grace which gives free access to God, and the freedom permitted of speaking on behalf of all saints and all men, remembering too past answers to prayer, surely in the consciousness of all this, thanksgivings

---

* The noun elsewhere occurs only in 1 Tim. iv. 5. The verb $\mathit{\unicode{x1F10}}\nu\tau\upsilon\gamma\chi\acute{\alpha}\nu\omega$ is used of the intercession of the Lord Jesus (Rom. viii. 34; Heb. vii. 25); of the Holy Ghost (Rom. viii. 27); of Elijah with God (Rom. xi. 2); and of the Jews with Festus against Paul (Acts xxv. 24).

might well mingle with supplications, prayers, and intercessions. How comprehensive then can prayers be, since we may pray for all saints and for all men! In Eph. vi. 18 we are exhorted to pray for all saints; in 1 Tim. ii. 1 we are taught to pray for all men. Each of these statements is in character with the epistle in which it occurs. In Ephesians we are taught especially about the body of Christ; in Timothy we have God presented as the Saviour. Prayer for all saints is in keeping with the teaching of the one; prayer for all men is in full accord with the line of truth in the other.

Living as the early Christians did under rulers who knew not God, they were taught that prayer was to be offered for those in authority, as well as for the well-being and necessities of individuals. Thus grace, of which they were partakers, was to be manifested in them; and a quiet and peaceable life, in all godliness and honesty might be lead, the result of God upholding and restraining the constituted authorities placed over them. Thank God, we in our land are little familiar with the troubles, and the insecurity to life and property, which are liable to attend the absence of a stable government. Still, prayer for the powers that be we should not on that account forget; for this is good and acceptable in the sight of God our Saviour, who will have all men to be saved, and to come to the knowledge of the truth. Of God's willingness to save *all* we are here reminded, that we may pray for all. How willing is God to save! He declares it, and He has given proofs of it: "There is one God, and one Mediator between God and men." Here national distinctions and dispensational position drop out of sight. And the Mediator, the Man Christ Jesus, gave Himself a ransom for all, and appointed Paul to be a herald, an apostle, and a teacher of nations, in faith and truth to testify of it. He gave Himself! What words for us to read! He has provided too the channel by which this should be made known. What desire on His part for men's salvation does this manifest! What freedom must this have given to Christians when presenting petitions to God!

CHAPTER XI.

WORSHIP.

TO worship God is the duty of every intelligent creature. The angels worship Him; His saints too worship Him; by and by all on earth will worship Him (Zeph. ii. 11; Isa. lxvi. 23). As God, He is the proper object of adoration for all His intelligent creatures, and men will be expected, in the terms of the everlasting gospel, to worship Him (Rev. xiv. 7). But whilst angels render Him homage in truth for what He is, unrenewed men too will worship Him, in millennial days, though only from having learnt His power in judgment, or from a desire to enjoy life on earth under the sway of the Lord Jesus Christ. Such outward homage, however, is not all that God would receive from men, for He desires the adoration of the *heart*. Hence worship of a different character, and springing from very different motives, God seeks and receives from His people on earth (John iv. 23). About this He has instructed us, telling us in His Word of the character, the power, and the true place of worship, as well as furnishing us therein with regulations for His saints when met in assembly for such a purpose.

But first, what is worship? It is the homage of the creature rendered to God. Hence the terms commonly used, both in Hebrew and Greek, to express it, have reference primarily to the action of the body as that by which worship is outwardly indicated; so that, although it may at times be but an external act of homage without the heart being really engaged in it (Zeph. ii. 11), the idea conveyed by the terms in frequent use indicates the occupation for the time being of the worshiper with an object outside of himself. Where the homage of the heart is rendered to God, the worshiper is of course rightly occupied with Him. Worship, then, differs from prayer in this, that in prayer we are occupied with the wants which we thereby present to God, whilst in worship we are occupied with God Himself. Hence true worship of God may take the form of praise, or thanksgiving, or both. If we praise Him, we tell out what He has discovered to us of Himself. If we thank Him, we speak of what He has done for us, or of what we have received from Him. In a certain sense His works praise Him, for they set forth something of what He is. But His saints bless Him, or speak well of Him; for they have received from Him (Psa. cxlv. 10). For fallen creatures to worship Him in truth, then, they must be partakers of His grace; for one conscious of his sinfulness and sins, and what such deserve from God, cannot really worship Him till saved by faith in Christ. Till then, such an one would be occupied with his condition and deserts, and not with God.

It was at that memorable interview by the well in Samaria that this subject was first opened up, by the Lord Himself, to a poor sinner, whose ways indicated that she had been far indeed in heart from God. And here we see how perfect in wisdom are God's ways. To Nicodemus, a man of reputation amongst the Jews, the Lord insisted on the necessity of the new birth. To the woman who had lost all character among men, He spoke of worship. The woman needed to be born again, and Nicodemus was to become a worshiper; but the teacher of Israel was taught his need, and the instrumentality by which it could be met; the woman was instructed in the pouring out of the heart in adoration to God, even the Father. This surely would not have been man's way with these two; but it was God's, and it was as perfect as it was fitting. For man to become a true worshiper he must be taught his need of grace, and his condition by nature. The convicted sinner is to understand, that the band of true worshipers is only recruited and enlarged from those who are indebted to the saving mercy of God. On this subject let us now enter, taking it up in the order indicated above.

First, then, as to the character of true worship. Having discovered from the Lord's knowledge of her life that she was in the presence of a prophet, the woman thereupon brought up the question which had been raised by the Samaritans with the Jews, whether at Jerusalem or at Gerizim men ought to worship. With her, as with many in this day, it was the opinion of men that she thought of. "Ye say that in Jerusalem is the place where men ought to worship." Not a word, be it observed, does she speak of God's will in the matter. Not a thought does she indicate of any choice Jehovah might have made, or any preference that He had shown for one place over another. Yet He had distinctly made choice of Jerusalem, He had clearly marked out mount Moriah as the mount of the Lord. David learnt that when God accepted the offering on Ornan's threshingfloor, by which the plague was effectually stopped in Israel (1 Chron. xxii. 1). Solomon was aware of God's choice when he began to build the temple (2 Chron. iii. 1), and God assured him, after its dedication, of the selection He had made of the place, having sanctified the house, that His name should be there forever (2 Chron. vii. 16). From this purpose God never receded. In the songs of degrees we read of it (Psa. cxxxii. 14). In Ezek. xliii. 7 we meet with Jehovah's settled purpose about it. In God's word, then, there was no uncertainty about it, though very likely the woman was in entire ignorance of the scriptures which speak of it. But whose fault was that? The position she was in, and that from her birth, and because of her birth, may have kept her from acquaintance with those portions of the divine revelation. This might and would explain how it was that she was ignorant; but it was no real excuse for that ignorance. She claimed to have relation with the God of Jacob, yet knew not, nor sought to learn, whether on this question He had revealed His mind in His Word. And this is clear from her way of introducing the subject; for, prophet though the Jewish stranger was in her eyes, she neither attempted to appeal to Scripture in support of the selection of Gerizim, nor did she ask Him what scriptural authority the Jews had for going up to Jerusalem. "Ye say," was her language. How many since her day have taken up similar language, when the question of worship has been brought before them! Yet at no time has that been in God's eyes an open question, since He was first pleased to instruct people about it.

"Our fathers worshiped in this mountain." That was true. For centuries the rival temple at Gerizim had been the centre of Samaritan worship. But that fact could add nothing in support of its claims to be the house of God. Granted that she was following in the footsteps of her fathers, worshiping as they had done before her, still the question remained, Was that place selected by God in which to rear up His sanctuary, and acceptable worship to be offered therein? One word from Scripture would outweigh all the claims of Gerizim, even if they had been enveloped in the prescriptive right of hoar antiquity. A "thus saith the Lord" would demolish, for subject minds, all arguments and reasoning of men.

Again. Assuming that she was in ignorance of the revelation about Jerusalem, was the worship offered at Gerizim, if done in ignorance, to be accepted of God? Granted too that many a Samaritan conscientiously resorted to that mountain, would worshiping God according to their conscience make it thereby acceptable in His eyes? Was man's conscience to override the plain direction of the Word? By no means. So the Lord disstinctly repudiated the claims of Gerizim, and the worship there carried on. "Ye worship ye know not what: we know what we worship: for salvation is of the Jews." The Samaritans were self-condemned, for out of Zion the Deliverer was to come (Psa. xiv. 7); from the stem of Jesse the King would spring (Isa. xi. 1). Their position apart from the Jews practically denied this. But more, they worshiped what they knew not. The Jewish prophet, as she thought Him, had now spoken, and demolished in a moment all the supposed claims of Gerizim. Those words, too, had surely a deep meaning, "Ye worship ye know not what." But was He authorized to speak in such a manner? She little thought that the stranger was *the* Prophet indeed (Deut. xviii. 18), and the only-begotten Son of God as well. How God then viewed the Samaritan position, politically and ecclesiastically, that woman learnt from Him whose house was the temple at Jerusalem. Now three things this interview distinctly settles for us. It is dangerous, as well as wrong, to make that a matter of man's opinion on which God has expressed His mind. Worshiping God as our fathers have done before us is no guarantee that we are worshiping aright; and granting that what we do is done with a good conscience, that is no ground for God to accept it. What God has said about worship, is the one important question when that subject comes up; to conform to His mind in the matter is the simple duty of His people.

On the positive teaching on this subject the Lord at once enters. On the divine choice of Jerusalem He does not dilate, for the question in connection with worship was assuming a new aspect. It would not be a question merely of locality, but of the Person worshiped, and of the character of worship. "Woman, believe me, the hour cometh, when ye shall neither in this mountain, nor yet at Jerusalem, worship the Father." Jerusalem would indeed be overthrown; the house there erected, at the cost of great labor and wealth, would be thrown down. Yet the Samaritans would not be able to triumph over the Jews; for in neither place, in the time coming, were men to worship the Father. "The Father!" Surely this must have struck her as new language. Israel was God's son, His firstborn (Ex. iv. 22), the children of the Lord their God (Deut. xiv. 1). Jehovah was a Father to Israel, and Ephraim was His firstborn (Jer. xxxi. 9). Yet they never had worshiped Him as the Father; for none can know the Father, except those to whom the Son will reveal Him (Matt. xi. 27). Now this is one essential feature of Christian worship. God known, in His relation to His people as their Father, and they worshiping Him as such; but this revelation is a matter for individuals—"he to whomsoever the Son will reveal Him." Each one, then, who knows the Father, is indebted for it to the Son of God; and only those who know Him, it is manifest, can worship Him. National worship, as such, then at once disappears; for if all in the nation could really worship God, it would be as His children, and not on the ground of nationality, since He stands in the relation of Father to all who on earth are now privileged to approach Him. How many a company of professing worshipers would be thinned at once, did all real Christians understand and maintain this simple truth.

But the Lord stopped not there. He proceeded to tell the woman the character of worship that would be acceptable to the Father. It must be in spirit and in truth. The nature of God, and the relation in which He stands to each true worshiper, must be understood, if we would worship Him aright. He is a Spirit, so we must worship Him in spirit and in truth; for it is in the consciousness that He is our Father, and as the Father, that we are permitted to pour out the heart to Him. "In spirit:" —then it must be spiritual in its character, and from that time no *formal* worship would God be willing to receive. The true worshipers must worship Him in spirit. What God is should teach us that. "In truth," too, must it be. Hence, the revelation He has vouchsafed, whatever it be, the worshiper must be acquainted with, and conform to. No going back then to the revelation of a former time and trying to worship Him on that ground will be worship in truth. So, now that the atoning work is accomplished, and that by one offering the Lord Jesus has perfected forever them that are sanctified, we cannot worship God aright if we seek to draw nigh without forgiveness enjoyed, and acceptance in Christ known. For entrance into the heavenly sanctuary is only enjoined after we have been taught that believers are sanctified by the will of God, are perfected by the one offering of Christ, and their sins and iniquities are remembered by God no more (Heb. x. 10, 14–22). Such then are the ones the

Father seeks to worship Him. Who would have thought this? The Father is seeking worshipers—men with hearts filled, free to empty themselves in His presence in the enjoyment of His grace, it is these the Father is seeking, and the Son assures us of it. It is joy to worship. What joy must it be to the Father to receive the worship of His children! What joy to the Father, the Son, and the Holy Ghost, as well as to God's children, when from the fulness of the heart they worship the Father! What misery resulted from the fall! What abounding joy springs from the atoning death of the Lord Jesus Christ!

With the mention of the *Person to be worshiped*, and the *character of true worship* (these both taught directly), and the class of people who can be worshipers (this taught indirectly from the Lord thus conversing with the woman), His instructions on this important question ended. Scripture, however, gives us more about it, and makes it very plain that true Christian worship is different from anything ever before known. Paul, once zealous for the law, brought up at the feet of Gamaliel, knew well what Judaism was, and the evil of Judaizing teaching in the Church of God. So, warning his beloved Philippians against such, he sets forth in a simple way the true Christian position in contrast with all such teaching. "We are the circumcision, who worship by the Spirit of God" (so we should read this clause), "and rejoice in Christ Jesus, and have no confidence in the flesh" (Phil. iii. 3). The Holy Ghost, then, is the power of true Christian worship. Now this was both new and distinctive. It characterized Christian worship then. It must characterize it still. We are to worship by the Spirit of God. Forms and ceremonies God gave to Israel, in conformity with which they worshiped Jehovah. Forms and ceremonies have *not* been given to us. We know not even the words in which the Lord gave thanks at the institution of the Supper. We have no description of an apostle breaking bread. We have not a single hymn, that we know of, which was in use in any Christian assembly in apostolic days. Nothing of this has been handed down to us in the Word. We have no book of Christian psalms; for we are to worship by the Spirit of God. Now if we go back to Old Testament forms, and mould Christian worship in conformity with them, we lose this distinctive feature of Christianity—worshiping by the Spirit of God.

And herein lies a danger arising from ignorance of dispensational teaching. It may seem very plausible to say we use scripture language, and can point to precedents in the Word for our ways in worship. But if Scripture is used unintelligently, and dispensational teaching is not known, the soul may be beguiled by using words of Scripture to surrender distinctive teaching of Christianity. This is a very serious matter, and one which concerns all Christians; for have not most of us had part in such confusion? But have all seen the evil of it? Do all understand what it is to worship by the Spirit of God, allowing Him, who is in the Assembly, to guide in worship when Christians meet together for that purpose?

Now the word of God takes such pains to point out the distinction between the two dispensations; whereas Christians, through ignorance of New Testament teaching, have practically sought to mingle them—attempting to put the wine of Christian truth into bottles of Jewish forms. The mistake of this, to say nothing more, is further apparent when we consider, thirdly, *what the place is* in which we now worship God. It is the sanctuary on high, into which the great Priest has entered by His own blood—a sanctuary into which Israel never had access, and never will. Now into the holiest are we permitted to enter "by the blood of Jesus, by a new and living way, which He hath consecrated for us, through the veil, that is to say, His flesh" (Heb. x. 19, 20). But for us to be there, three things are requisite. The Lord Jesus must have died, else the veil could not have been rent; atonement by His blood must have been made, otherwise we should not have boldness to enter in, nor have known of a living way into the presence-chamber of God; and, thirdly, those only can enter in without judgment overtaking them, who acknowledge the death of Christ to be their ground and way of entry into the holiest. It is, then, both a new and a living way, and the only one that God has ever sanctioned for those who have sinned against Him. "Through the veil, that is to say, His flesh." None, then, are entitled to draw nigh who do not own the atoning death of Christ to be their way of entrance there.

Now this is an important point; for thus carefully does God guard the way into His presence. The veil was rent, and through it, as rent, we pass into the holiest. Had God removed it before the Lord had died, anybody might get into His presence, whether owning the Lord's death or not; for what barred the way into the holiest would have barred it no longer. But we go through it, as it were, because rent by the Lord's death upon the cross. None, then, who refuse to acknowledge His death as their way of entry can ever get in there. To all who do, there is no barrier now; to those who do not, there is no way into the divine presence by which they can enter and be sheltered from judgment.

But all this is in direct contrast with Judaism. Atonement by blood not really made, the way into the holiest not yet manifested, the veil intact—these were characteristic features of Jewish worship. Atonement *made*, the veil *rent*, through which, by the blood of Jesus, we approach God—these are features of true Christian worship. And the mention of them is enough to make any see at a glance that acceptable worship now must be very different in its characteristics from acceptable worship of old. An *earthly* sanctuary, too, they had. Into the *heavenly* one we enter; hence the language of saints in heaven (Rev. v.) is the language we can take up now. And further, as there is no altar of burnt-offering in heaven, nor are sacrificial victims there offered up, so we approach not now to an altar, nor do we present any sacrificial victims to God. We worship in person on earth as we shall worship in heaven by and by, except that now in these bodies, with sin within us, and the world around us, we are often distracted in thought when we should have the mind wholly concentrated on Him we are worshiping. But Israel will again approach the altar of burnt-offering, and bring their victims with them, because they will worship in the earthly sanctuary, with which such a service is inseparably connected. We do neither, because we worship in the holiest in heaven, and, according to the tabernacle order, have left the altar behind us.

Thus it was that the Christian assembly, met for worship, was to conduct itself in a manner very different from that of the congregation of Israel. The latter had priests and Levites to do the service at the altar and in the tabernacle, or temple; but all believers now are priests. There are no true worshipers who are not priests; for though sacrificial service at the altar has for us ceased, spiritual sacrifices we do offer up, even praise and thanksgivings to God. Had we then visited the service in the temple, and then looked in on an assembly gathered together for worship in accordance with the direction given us through the apostle Paul, how great would have been the difference! Both would have called themselves the people of the Lord; but the latter would have let us know that they were individually children of God. In the temple we should have seen a marked difference between the sexes. The men had a place to which no woman had access; and the notice, warning a Gentile of death if he obtruded himself into the court of the males, would have met us probably full in the face. In the Christian assembly there would have been seen no such separation of sexes, nor any distinction of races: those once Jews, with those once Gentiles, would have been seen together worshiping God. And whereas in the temple we might have witnessed sacrificial rites to deal with sins committed, in the assembly we should have heard sacrifices of praise and thanksgivings for sins forgiven, atonement accomplished, and redemption known and enjoyed. Had we asked a Jew for the house of God, he would have directed us to the temple on mount Moriah; but on visiting it, we should not have found God there present, for He did not dwell in it after the Babylonish captivity. Had we asked a Christian for the house of God, he would have told us of the Assembly of the living God (1 Tim. iii. 15); and going to it, we might have learnt, through the instrumentality of any brother exercising his gift at the moment, that God was among them (1 Cor. xiv. 25). The temple, we should have found, was desolate; but God was present in the Assembly.

Surveying the company gathered together, no president would have been discernible; yet, if all were subject to the guidance of the Holy Spirit, no disorder would have been perceived. Order would have reigned, not because they had drawn up a set of human rules, or had instituted a hierarchy of human appointment,—for neither the one nor the other had a place in the Assembly at the beginning,—but gathered unto the name of the Lord Jesus Christ, His presence would have been owned, and the guidance of the Holy Ghost in every act of worship distinctly recognized. As the meeting went on, hearts full of grace enjoyed would have poured themselves out in worship, either by one voice expressing the common feelings of the assembly, or by a hymn raised and sung with heartiness by all. The notes of praise having died away, silence would perhaps have reigned till broken by the voice of another speaking to edification, exhortation, or comfort. Not a word uttered for show, not a thing done but what the Spirit of God directed; no haste in taking part in the guidance of the assembly in worship, nor interruption of any speaker, would have been seen; for the Spirit of God never acts out of season. And though all the males might prophesy, not too many would have done it, lest the profit of some or all might have been marred. Further, no prophet would have been observed to speak as if impelled by a divine influence which he could not resist, for "the spirits of the prophets are subject to the prophets;" and no one would have opened his mouth in a tongue unless there was some one to interpret. The women would have been silent, save when the strain of a hymn permitted them to join in concert, or the responsive Amen could fittingly come from the heart and lips. And, what would surely have struck one accustomed to the synagogue or temple, whilst the women had their heads covered, the men would have been seen with theirs uniformly uncovered (1 Cor. xi.).

Now, is this an ideal picture? Let the reader study 1 Cor. xiv., and see if the mark has been overstepped; for in it we have the Spirit of God correcting, by the apostle, disorders which had appeared in the Corinthian assembly, and telling them likewise what was admissible, as well as what was forbidden, in the assemblies of God's saints. Shall Scripture in this, as in other things, be our guide, or the rules and regulations devised by the wit of men? "If any man think himself to be a prophet, or spiritual, let him acknowledge (or recognize) that the things that I write unto you are the commandments of the Lord" (1 Cor. xiv. 37). Thus wrote the apostle Paul. Have these injunctions and directions been superseded by a more recent divine revelation? Can they lose their force by the lapse of time, or the change of locality? (1 Cor. i. 2; xiv. 33.) Are they not for our guidance, whenever and wherever Christians are gathered in assembly for worship, in this the twentieth century as much as they were in the first? "The hour now is," said the Lord, "when the true worshipers shall worship the Father in spirit and in truth" (John iv. 23).

CHAPTER XII.

THE INSTITUTION OF THE SUPPER.

"THEY continued stedfastly in the apostle's doctrine and fellowship, in breaking of bread and in prayers" (Acts ii. 42). Such is the sacred historian's brief account of the ways of the first converts to Christianity after the day of Pentecost. The company in which they were found, and the teaching to which they were subject, these are classed together. Then, as a consequence, we learn of the religious exercises which characterized them, viz., the breaking of bread and prayers; for by the omission of the conjunction *and* before "breaking of bread" in accordance with the reading of the best MSS., that and prayer are stated as characteristic actions of the Christian community. Here, then, for the first time after the institution of the Supper, do we read of the Christians meeting to break bread together in remembrance of the Lord's death; and from henceforth this peculiar Christian service is called the breaking of bread (Acts xx. 7, 11) as well as the Lord's Supper (1 Cor. xi. 20). By the latter term we are reminded by whom it was instituted; by the former, is expressed the action of those who partake of it.

Yet the action in itself was nothing new. With the simple meaning of the term the Jews were certainly familiar (Matt. xiv. 19; xv. 36; Mark viii. 6, 19; Lam. iv. 4); nor were they strangers to the custom of breaking bread and drinking wine with mourners to comfort them. Of this Jeremiah writes (xvi. 7). (The marginal reading of the authorized version conveys what the Hebrew original expresses.) What, however, was new, and peculiar too, was the interpretation the Lord gave to His act of breaking bread.

To comfort mourners for the dead, their friends, we learn, would break bread for them, and give them the cup of consolation for their father or their mother. It was all that friendship could do when death had entered the family and bereavement pressed heavily on the sorrowing ones. Sweet, doubtless, such sympathy had often proved itself to be, as the loving care of friends thus displayed itself in the house, and on the day of sorrow; but sweet as it might be, the heart's ache could not thereby be removed, nor the void which death had caused be thereby filled. But who could comfort the disciples for the death of their Master and Lord? No friends could be found to do it; and worse than that, the world's enmity they were about to experience in a way they had never felt it before. Yet a comfort, but far more than a comfort, would they find in breaking bread together in remembrance of the Lord's death; for whilst friends might give to bereaved ones the cup of consolation, the disciples received from the hands of Christ Himself the cup of blessing. And yet more; for His death was their gain, how great soever was their sorrow in losing Him. Now, indeed, the thought was new that the death of one could be productive of real, everlasting gain to others; yet so it was in the case of the Lord's death, though in His only. This the disciples were to remember, and in the presence of the memorials of it to give thanks as they acknowledged it.

Of the institution of the Lord's Supper we have four inspired accounts. Matthew, Mark and Luke tell us about it; and Paul, addressing the Corinthians, acquaints them with that which he had received direct from the Lord in glory concerning it (1 Cor. xi. 23). When, and where, the apostle of the Gentiles received it we are not told; but the fact that he did receive it direct from the Lord, years after He had ascended to the right hand of the Majesty on high, testifies of the desire that all His people, whether gathered out from Jews or from Gentiles, should equally, and in the same manner, announce His death till He come. Of these four accounts, one only is from the pen of an eye-witness, and a recipient of the elements from the Lord in person. As, however, we examine the four accounts, we have to confess that we should have lost something had any one of them been missing.

Had Matthew's account been lost, we should not have known that the Lord, in giving the cup, said, "Drink ye all of it;" had that of Mark not survived to our day, we should not have known that they did all drink of it (Mark xiv. 23). Communion in one kind was not practised in the Lord's presence, nor sustained by anything that fell from His lips. Again, Matthew, the eye-witness, has also recorded other words not met with elsewhere. "For the remission of sins" is an addition only found in this connection in his Gospel. Now, comparing Jeremiah xxxi. 31-34 with the four accounts of the Supper, we trace an important connection. Of all the Old Testament writers, Jeremiah is the only one who mentions the new covenant, though other prophets describe blessings to be enjoyed under it. The Lord is the first person in the New Testament who speaks of it, and He supplies an important link with reference to it. Jeremiah predicted the new covenant, and the blessings to be enjoyed under it, viz., the knowledge of God, and the forgiveness of sins; but he did not state on what sacrifice this covenant would be based. This the Lord did when He uttered the words, "This is My blood of the new covenant, which is shed for many for the remission of sins" (Matt. xxvi. 28). Thus His words, when giving the cup to His disciples, naturally recall to our mind the passage in Jeremiah, and show us that He revealed what the prophet could not; and when we remember the dispensational character of Matthew's Gospel, presenting, as it does, the Lord as Son of David, and Son of Abraham, is there not a propriety in the fullest reference to that covenant which concerns directly God's earthly people, being found in the Gospel which, more than any of the others, presents the Lord in His special relation to them? Forgiveness of sins we enjoy now, and they will by and by; but they will only know it as part of the blessings of the new covenant, and when that covenant shall have been made with them. We who believe know it now, because the blood on which it will rest has been shed; so the blessing, based on the atoning work of the Lord, can be shared in by us whilst the Lord is in heaven.

Turning to Luke's account, we learn what the other two Evangelists do not make plain—how distinct was the Lord's Supper from the paschal feast, though both were partaken of by the disciples at the same table, and on the same night. His account of the paschal feast is given us in chap. xxii. 15–18; his account of the institution of the Supper follows in verses 19, 20. At the paschal feast the Lord had His place as one with them; at the Supper He was, as it were, the host, dispensing that which He had provided to those who were the guests. How much, surely, we should have lost had Luke's account not seen the light, or had it perished by the carelessness or hostility of man to the truth! for it is the beloved Physician who has given us to understand that the Lord prized the opportunity of observing the Passover—"With desire I have desired to eat this Passover with you before I suffer." Matthew, who must have heard these words, has not repeated them. Luke, who certainly was not present, alone records them; and fitly does he do it, since the manhood of the Lord Jesus Christ comes out especially in his Gospel. How the Lord Jesus, as one of Israel, viewed the Passover these words show us, and surely afford us instruction as to the light in which we should view the privilege and the opportunity of now commemorating His death, which, when Israel shall enjoy the fruits of it, will cause them to relegate to a second place God's memorable intervention in the past (Jer. xxiii. 7, 8). God's intervention was in the Lord's eyes no light thing. How we who sit at His table view redemption by His blood may well be a question when His words above quoted come before us.

Further, we learn from Luke's account of what passed in that upper room, that though the Lord partook of the Passover, He did not drink of the paschal cup, which, it would seem, had been handed to Him; for the historian wrote, "Having received a cup,"* not "having taken it," as our English translation would intimate. Now, in the original regulations about the Passover there is no mention of a cup; and, as Deut. xvi. 3–8 shows us, there was originally no room for it; for the character of the feast in the month of Abib, as that chapter teaches us, was not one of joy; and no joy is mentioned as characteristic of

---

* $\delta\varepsilon\xi\alpha\mu\varepsilon\nu o\varsigma$, "having received," is the word used by Luke of the paschal cup; $\lambda\alpha\mu\beta\acute{\alpha}\nu\omega$ is the verb used by all of the Supper.

a Jewish festival till the time arrived for keeping the Feast of Weeks, when, in the possession of the fruits of resurrection in the land, they were to rejoice (Deut. xvi. 11). What, then, God had instituted, to that the Lord conformed. Of that which man had added the Lord did not partake. He did not, however, condemn the introduction of the cup as wrong; but the time for joy in connection with full redemption not having come, He did not drink of it Himself, though, when He had given thanks, He handed it to His disciples to divide amongst themselves, saying, "I will not drink of the fruit of the vine until the kingdom of God shall come." Thus far we have Luke's account of the paschal feast. What follows is that of the supper.

This is an entirely new service, quite distinct from any of which Israel as such had been allowed to partake; but one in which all the children of God, of whatever nationality, are privileged to have part. What then is the character of this service? and what the meaning of it? Both these questions are answered by the Lord Himself. His action tells us of the one, His words teach us about the other. "He gave thanks." Then the service is eucharistic indeed; for that was all we are told that He did before He brake the bread, and gave it to the disciples. And a second time He gave thanks before He handed to them the cup of which they were to drink. That He gave thanks before handing the cup, Luke and Paul imply; but Matthew and Mark expressly state it. Agreeing in this, they agree also in stating that He "blessed" (εὐλογήσας) before He broke the bread, whereas Luke and Paul affirm He "gave thanks" (εὐχαριστήσας). The difference is not great, and admits probably of this explanation, that whilst the two latter give the character of

His utterance, the others express the form in which it came forth. A eucharistic service then is that of the breaking of bread. He gave thanks, but in what terms we know not. Matthew, who must have heard it, is silent upon it; neither Mark, nor Luke, nor Paul have supplied the omission. It must have been a wonderful thanksgiving when the Lord gave thanks to God for the results of His atoning death, so soon to be an accomplished fact. Who on earth could enter into them as He could? Who knew like Him what the judgment of God was? Who but Himself could then understand what are the joys of the Father's love, and the Father's house? Full and perfect then must that thanksgiving have been; yet not a syllable of it has been preserved in God's book. And rightly so; for since the Spirit of God is to direct us in our worship, the words of the Lord on that occasion have been carefully kept from us; and nowhere have we even the thanksgiving utterances of an apostle when breaking bread at the Lord's table. Had it been otherwise, would not such have been used as a form? and no service at the Lord's table would have been thought complete without them. But then dependence on the Holy Spirit's guidance would have been really surrendered. Wisely, therefore, have the terms of the Lord's thanksgiving been omitted from the account of His institution of the supper.

Are we on this account placed at a disadvantage? No; for we know what the character of the service is to be, and we know too, from the Lord's action, how perfect in His eyes is His atoning work; for as He gave thanks, and that only, at the institution of the supper, we are taught that nothing needed to be, nothing could be, added to the value of the sacrificial work He was about to offer as propitiation for the sins of the people. No word have we here of prayer. What room could there be to ask for anything in the contemplation of accomplished atonement? Prayer may come in after the breaking of bread has taken place, as those gathered together think of saints unable to be present, or of souls still unsaved, or of anything else in connection with the Lord's work or God's purposes; but prayer in the place of thanksgiving, when met to break bread, is assuredly not in harmony with the Lord's ways at His table; for the work is a perfect work, a finished work, as Scripture affirms (Heb. x. 14–18), and the Lord's own action of giving thanks abundantly confirms.

The character of the service thus expressed, its meaning too, was explained by Him when He handed to His disciples first the bread, and then the wine—"This is My body, which is given for you;" "this cup is the new covenant in My blood, which is shed for you." What grace is expressed in these words, "My body given for you!" None could have lawfully demanded His death. "He made himself," said the Jews when delivering him to Pilate, "the Son of God, and by our law he ought to die." But He was, and is, the Son of God. None then could lawfully have demanded His death, though the Jews condemned Him as guilty of blasphemy, and accused Him of high treason to Pilate the governor. His statement about His person was true, and Pilate acquitted Him of any charge of which he could take cognizance. Yet He died. His body was given for us. He surrendered Himself. His blood was shed for us. Did God keep back anything that was for man's good? The devil had persuaded Adam and Eve that He did. Now what an answer has God given to that!—an answer such

THE INSTITUTION OF THE SUPPER. 131

as no man could have expected, and one of which the devil then could have had no foreknowledge. For the death of His Son on the cross, not for man merely, but for sinners, was to be the overwhelming, the touching proof that God would withhold nothing of which we had need. "He spared not His own Son, but delivered Him up for us all," writes Paul to believers at Rome (Rom. viii. 32). "He sent His Son," writes John, "to be the propitiation for our sins" (1 John iv. 10). Nor this only: the Son gave Himself, as Paul has taught us (Gal. i. 4; ii. 20; 1 Tim. ii. 6; Titus ii. 14); but the apostle was not the first who declared that. The Son Himself announced it (Matt. xx. 28; Mark x. 45; John vi. 51). The joy was His of declaring in plain words that He would surrender Himself to die, to glorify God and to save sinners.

In Matthew and Mark we read of His blood shed "for *many*." In Luke it is "for *you*." This makes the announcement more personal and pointed; and he is the only one of the four who tells us that the Lord spake thus, both at the giving of the bread and at the giving of the cup. Were the eleven then distressed at the prospect of His death? How fully would He comfort them by the institution of the Supper. They were never to forget His death, yet their remembrance of it would have no tinge of sadness in it. It would give joy to their hearts; for atonement and redemption were effected by it, and forgiveness and justification flowed from it, all of which they would learn after that the Holy Ghost should have come to set forth its blessed results, and to teach them and us of what the Lord's presence on high is the witness.

Learning then, as they must have done from the Lord's lips, what He thought of atonement by His blood, they also were taught how He would have them remember Him: "This do in remembrance of Me." Here again we are reminded that God's thoughts are not as our thoughts. Men love to dwell on great and noble deeds of others done in their life. The Lord's people were especially to remember Him in His death, and as dead; for the bread and the wine recall Him as actually dead: the former being the symbol of His body, and the latter of His blood, which in the supper is viewed as distinct from His body. Hence communion in one kind is a denial of the Lord's death, for it regards the blood as not shed. It virtually presents Him to us as alive before death: in which case atonement has not been wrought—there is no forgiveness for our sins (Heb. ix. 22), and the Lord abides alone (John xii. 24).

But not only were those who had been with Him on earth thus to remember Him; all His people, from that day till the Church shall be taken, are in the same manner to remember Him. His enemies in the world would rejoice that He was dead (John xvi. 20), hoping thereby to have got rid forever of Him whom they contemptuously called "that deceiver" (Matt. xxvii. 63), little knowing that they had, by their rejection of the Christ, paved the way for the appearance by and by of "*the* deceiver" indeed, the Antichrist (2 John 7). All the Lord's people too, after He had risen again, would rejoice that He had died, reaping as they would the abiding fruits of His atoning death—sanctification, forgiveness, justification, and entrance into the holiest by His blood.

But when, and how often they were thus to remember Him, the Lord does not specify in His Word. We gather from it, however, *when* they met for that purpose, viz., on the first day of the week (Acts xx. 7). At first it may have been that they broke bread together each day. Afterwards, it certainly was done on the first day of the week, and for that special purpose did they at Troas assemble together. Prayer, preaching, teaching, are all useful and needful, but they do not supersede the necessity of meeting to break bread. When thus met there may be room for teaching. The Lord, after the breaking of bread, spoke what we have in John xiv., if not also what is stated in chaps. xv., xvi. And Paul at Troas discoursed for a long time when the company were assembled for the breaking of bread. Yet, the purpose for which they came together was not to hear Paul, but to show the Lord's death. Bearing this in mind, we shall not go to the Lord's table to hear some gifted teacher, but to break bread in remembrance of the Lord Jesus Christ. Gift or no gift will make no difference as to the motive which will take us to that meeting. We shall go to remember Him who once entered into death to save us. Edification by gift, all should be thankful for; but the absence of it will keep none away from the table who know for what reason we are to assemble.

And how often can we thus meet? No limit is placed to this; and a word of the Lord, only preserved by Paul, makes this clear: "This do ye, as oft as ye drink it, in remembrance of Me."* At what period of the day should we break bread? some may ask. This too is left an open question. The supper was instituted in the evening. They met on that occasion at Troas at night. Probably the Corinthians too came together when the day had declined (1 Cor. xi. 21); for the term $\delta\epsilon\hat{\imath}\pi\nu o\nu$, translated

---

* "The word translated *remembrance* has an active signification of 'recalling,' or 'calling to mind,' as a memorial. 'For the calling Me to mind.'"—Note, in *New Trans. of the N. T. by J. N. D.*

there *supper*, is not used in the New Testament of a morning meal. In Luke xiv. 12 it is clearly used of the meal which succeeded dinner. But no rule is laid down as to the hour when we are to break bread, though the first day of the week is marked out as the one specially suited for that, on grounds which all can readily understand. How often besides Christians may break bread, is left to the Lord's people as they may be guided.

And now, ere concluding this article, a little verse, found only in Matt. (xxvi. 30) and Mark (xiv. 26), but word for word the same in both, must receive a moment's attention: "And when they had sung a hymn, they went out into the Mount of Olives." If ever there was an occasion on which common sorrow might have outweighed common joy at the remembrance of the shelter from divine judgment by blood, it would have been on that evening when the Lord ate the last Passover with His disciples. But instead of that, ere they left the upper-room they sung together to God; a hint for us, that no sorrow of whatever character is to override the heart's joy which flows from the remembrance of redemption. Their sorrow on losing the Lord was great (John xvi. 6), and He knew it; but their joy, as they recalled God's interposition on behalf of Israel, was nevertheless to be expressed. So surely should it be with us. Troubles and sorrows, whether individual or otherwise, are not to be allowed to outweigh the common joy, when we meet to show the Lord's death.

Thus far we have been considering scriptures which tell us why we should break bread, and how we should do it. Other scriptures give us practical teaching in connection with it. A consideration of these must be reserved for the following paper.

CHAPTER XIII.

PRACTICAL TEACHING IN CONNECTION WITH THE BREAKING OF BREAD.

OF the five apostles who wrote the Epistles three refer to the breaking of bread; viz., Peter, Jude, and Paul. Four of them were present at its institution. Paul was not; but he alone of the five gives us teaching in connection with it. Thus we learn that there is more instruction which flows from it than at first sight might appear, and that it is in part closely connected with the special revelation made known to Paul concerning the Church of God. As sitting at the Lord's table, the question of communion and association is necessarily raised: eating of the supper, the spirit in which we should partake of it, is not overlooked by the Lord. The first of these questions is taken up in 1 Cor. x.; the other is dealt with in the chapter that follows.

Having just emerged from idolatry, as was the case with the Corinthian Christians, some had seen the inanity of the idol, but had not apprehended the character of their new associations. In this they were not singular. There is often an interval of time, from whatever cause we need not here inquire, between the discovery of the evil from which souls may have separated, and the clear apprehension of the position, and its attendant responsibilities, into which they have been brought. As long as such a state continues, it is clear that steadiness of walk need not be expected. Hence the mistake of simply occupying people with protesting against that which is evil.

More is wanted than this, without however in the least undervaluing it; for there is the ceasing to do evil, and the learning to do well, with both of which a Christian, to be "throughly furnished unto all good works," must become acquainted.

Now some of the Corinthians knew that an idol was nothing in the world, and that there was none other God but one (1 Cor. viii. 4); yet they thought, if they discerned that, they might sit at meat in an idol's temple. In this they were wrong; and the apostle corrects their mistake. Care for their weaker brethren should have made them keep aloof from all participation, even only externally, in idolatrous rites (viii. 10–12). But more than this, they had no business to be there at all. The liberty for which some might plead, on the ground that they had discernment about the idol, should have been held in check by consideration for the weak brother's conscience. The question of being there at all, however, was settled forever by their having a place at the Lord's table and participating in the Lord's Supper. Granted that the idol was nothing; yet behind it were demons; and by sitting at meat at the idol's festival they would be having communion with demons. Was that a fitting thing for those who bore the name of Christ? "I would not," said the apostle, "that ye should have fellowship with demons" (x. 20). To drink of the cup of the Lord and the cup of demons, or be partakers of the Lord's table and the table of demons was impossible. "Ye cannot drink the cup of the Lord and the cup of demons," wrote the indignant apostle: "ye cannot be partakers of the Lord's table and of the table of demons" (x. 21). But in that way, this subject was obviously clear. The Lord and demons were antagonistic. A man could not have fellowship with both. Those in danger of outward conformity to heathen rites had never viewed the question in this light. How much light a word may cast upon a point! The Lord and demons! Between these there was no communion. Between them no man could form a connecting-link; yet a Christian, if unwatchful, might have fellowship with demons (ver. 20). Solemn thought! How it has been in Christendom sadly exemplified!

But he sets other considerations before them. "The cup of blessing which we bless, is it not the communion of the blood of Christ? The bread which we break, is it not the communion of the body of Christ?" What could the cup of demons give them? Nothing good. Of what did the cup of the Lord witness? Blessing purchased by His blood for those who had sinned against God, but who now believed on His name. With what had they communion at the Lord's Supper but with the body and blood of Christ? Speaking as to wise men, this should have been enough to open their eyes to the incongruity and the sinfulness of sitting at meat in an idol's temple. Observe, he here mentions the blood before the body of Christ—an inversion of the natural and the historical order in which they were first mentioned. Now since those to whom he wrote had once been worshiping idols, and had been mixed up with all the vileness and the debasing habits that idolatry encouraged, from all which they had been set free, and all their sins had been blotted out by the blood of Christ, how could they, remembering whose blood had been shed for them, and at what a cost they had been redeemed—how could they turn back to that from which they had been delivered? We can see, then, in the circumstances of the case, a reason for giving precedence on this occasion to the mention of the blood.

Besides this, he reminds them of that which the partaking the one loaf sets forth, viz., that all Christians are one body. We become members of this one body by the baptism of the Holy Ghost. We give practical expression to it by partaking of the one loaf. Independent action, therefore, is evil. If they belonged to one body, as they declared they did, how could they be identified with that which certainly was alien to it?

Several important principles are set forth, then, in these few verses. First, that one who has a place at the table must keep aloof from participation in that which God abhors. It is not a question, "What am I free to do?" but "What are the associations in which I have part?" Communion of the blood and body of Christ—is this what we profess and really enjoy? Then association with that which is opposed to God must not be an open question, nor a matter of indifference. From all idolatrous associations we must keep aloof; and keeping before us the principle thus illustrated, we must surely abstain from having communion with such evils as the Lord's word declares disqualifies those having part in them from being in the company of His people.

Secondly, breaking bread together, we confess, however little we may be aware of the character of our action, that we are part of one body with all other Christians; "for we being many are one body and one bread (or loaf), for we are all partakers of that one bread (or loaf)." Not that a body is thereby formed, but its existence is acknowledged and its oneness practically confessed; for there is but one Lord's table, how many soever may be the places in which saints are gathered unto Christ's name. The apostle at Ephesus and the saints at Corinth were members of one body. They owned it in doctrine, and confessed it week after week, as they broke bread in remembrance of the Lord Jesus Christ. From this body we cannot get free, nor by any declaration of independence discharge ourselves from responsibility in connection with it. Denominational ground is thereby condemned, for there is but one body, and in breaking bread together we declare it. But there is another side to this question. If we are all one body, we cannot be indifferent to the walk and the doctrine of those with whom we thus declare our oneness; for are we, as Christians having communion with His body and His blood, to be identified with acts and tenets which the Lord abhors? Care, and if need be discipline, becomes imperative when this truth of the one body is understood; for no choice is left us as to whether we will have this doctrine as an article of our creed or not. We cannot break bread together without confessing it.

Thirdly, as those at the Lord's table professedly participate in the result of the atoning work of Christ, none but Christians in truth have a place at it; for the Lord's Supper does not give life, but it is for all who have everlasting life, unless for the time being under the exercise of church-discipline. Eating Christ's flesh (by faith, of course) and drinking Christ's blood (John vi. 53, 54) gives life; eating of the Supper does not. As the bread from heaven, the Lord presents Himself to the world (John vi. 33, 51); but the Supper was instituted only for disciples. If the Supper could give life, those of whom Peter (2 Peter ii. 13) and Jude (12) wrote would have had it. None, however, should eat of the Supper who have not by faith first eaten of His flesh and drunk of His blood: for who have part now in the blessed results of His death but those who believe on Him? To the Lord's table, then, baptism by water can give no admittance, though none unbaptized ought to be seated thereat. For an unconverted person to sit there and partake of the bread and of the wine is a solemn thing, since he professes by his act that which is not true of his condition.

Further, as the table is the Lord's, all those at it are responsible to own and serve Him. Hence, too, the assembly should be watchful that it admits not, through inadvertence or carelessness, those who, as far as discernment can be exercised, are not Christians in truth; for admission to the table is the act of the assembly, and not that of an individual or individuals. On the other hand, to put away is also the act of the assembly, and for that, unquestionable proof should be adduced about the person dealt with, that he ought not to sit down with the saints. Surmise or suspicion will not be sufficient. Judas was reckoned with the twelve till his own act showed what he was.

Lastly, class distinction for the administering of the elements is seen to be foreign to the word of God. "The cup of blessing which we bless," writes the apostle. "The bread which we break." The blessing and the breaking are acts in common, though done by one as the mouthpiece and agent of the rest. Clericalism has no place at this table. To the Lord it belongs, and He is present where two or three are gathered unto His name. Who of men would dream of presiding where the Lord Himself is present? *At His table we are all guests.*

Now nothing like this table had ever been known before. It is true that a Jew could speak of Jehovah's table (Ezek. xli. 22; xliv. 16; Mal. i. 7, 12), for both the golden altar and the altar of burnt-offering are thus designated by the prophets, since on the altar Jehovah's portion was placed. But in the New Testament the Lord's table is the place at which He dispenses to all believers the memorials of His death. At the table of the Lord, of which the prophets write, no man sat. At the Lord's table, of which Paul writes, Christians have their place. Hence, once there, examination, or proving oneself ($\delta o \varkappa \iota \mu \acute{\alpha} \zeta \varepsilon \iota \nu$), becomes every Christian; he is not to stay away, but to *judge himself* ($\delta \iota \alpha \varkappa \rho \acute{\iota} \nu \varepsilon \iota \nu$), and so to eat of the bread and to drink of the cup. Now in this the Corinthians had failed. Meeting together to partake of the Lord's Supper, after or at a meal provided for all as was the custom, (of itself a beautiful expression of Christian fellowship) self had come in, alas; cliques had arisen; and instead of sitting together at a common table, where solemnity and grace should mark the meeting, each ate his *own* supper, the rich eating and drinking even to excess, while the poorer were left ashamed and hungry.

Thus the assembly of God was despised, and in the place where no differences should have been seen, the poor were put to shame. The disorder was grievous; it was scandalous (xi. 21, 22), and the Lord had already strongly marked His disapproval of it (xi. 30). How did the apostle deal with it? He reminded them that "the Lord Jesus, in the night in which He was delivered up, took bread; and having given thanks, brake it, and said, This is My body, which is for you: this do in remembrance of Me. In like manner also the cup, after having supped, saying, This cup is the new testament [or covenant] in My blood: this do, as oft as ye shall drink it, in remembrance of Me. For as often as ye shall eat this bread, and drink the cup, ye announce the death of the Lord until He come" (xi. 23–26). Simple, but surely heart-searching, must this statement have been; a quiet, but how great, a rebuke to their ways at the table. The Lord, their Lord, on the night of His betrayal, fully conscious of all that was before Him, thought of His people, and instituted this Supper for them. Should, then, disciples of that Lord be thinking of themselves, and allowing flesh thus to work, when they met to show His death? How could they, and at such a time! The professed purpose of their meeting should have rebuked all the disorders they had permitted and indulged in.

The Lord had died. But why? They well knew, and we know. He was delivered for our offenses. Then at His table, at His Supper, was the last place where self should have been unrestrained, unjudged; and we should observe how the apostle endeavors to impress this on them, and to keep it before them. Recapitulating that which he had received of the Lord about the Supper, Paul omits certain words with which we are made familiar by the Evangelists. "Take, eat" are, according to the best authorities, to be left out. "Drink ye all of it," it will be seen, has no place in Paul's account of what the Lord said about the cup. The word "broken," too, in in verse 24,—not found in any Evangelist in this connection,—we may be pretty sure, is an addition for which there is no scripture warrant.

Now there is a significance in the omission of, "Take, eat," in this recital of the institution of the Supper; for the apostle evidently was divinely directed not to fix their thoughts so much on the privilege which was theirs, as to impress on them the solemnity of what they were engaged in. Hence he simply writes, "This is My body, which is for you," fixing their attention, and ours likewise, on that of which the bread is the emblem; and the same with the cup. Surely as they read these words, and understood their import, a sense of shame must have come over them—remembering the scenes they had witnessed, in which some had openly had part. And what must still further have impressed them were the words peculiar to Paul—"For as often as ye shall eat this bread, and drink the cup, ye announce the death of the Lord until He come." How little soever they had been conscious of it, that was professed by the breaking of bread. He who is the Lord, the highest in dignity in creation, had died; and yet in the presence of the memorials of His death they had been unsolemnized! What brought Him to die? Sin,—their sins. On no other occasion then could they have been better or more forcibly reminded of what sin is in God's sight: and yet what had been their conduct at such a time! From what a nature, then, could this proceed! But were they worse than others? Alas! we all have the same evil nature; and though from circumstances drunkenness or gluttony could not be indulged in at the table in these days, self may be just as active in many other ways. What grace to provide atonement for such wretched creatures as by nature we are!

"The Lord's death." Such words invite meditation; they take us back to the past—"till He come." This carries us on in thought to the future. Partaking of the Supper they announced the Lord's death, and that in view of His return. The Lord had died, but the Lord will return; and He has lost none of His rights by death. In this He stands out alone from all that have entered into death. All that was His in this world before the cross is His now, and will be claimed by Him by and by. What was His by birth (Psa. ii.) is His still, and He will possess it, though He has died. But is this all that we have to think of as we announce the Lord's death? Oh, no! for by it all our blessings for eternity have been purchased, and are put beyond the reach of uncertainty. The mercies of David are made sure, because He is risen (Acts xiii. 34). Atonement, too, has been made by His blood shed on the cross; and the whole question of sin will by and by be openly proved to have been dealt with by His death (Heb. ix. 27, 28; John i. 29). He has tasted death for everthing; He has annulled by His death him that had the power of death; delivered them who through fear of death were all their lifetime subject to bondage; and has made propitiation for the sins of the people (Heb. ii.). Earth is concerned in His death, and far more than earth. How much results from the Lord's death which His people are privileged to announce.

The Supper, then, was no common meal. To partake of it unworthily was no light matter. He that did so was guilty concerning the body and blood of the Lord; *i. e.*, liable to judgment because of the slight thus put upon Him. Such a one ate and drank judgment to himself (κρίμα; not damnation, κατάκριμα) from not discerning the Lord's body—*i. e.* what the bread signified. The Lord's body here has no reference to the Church; and Paul never called the Church by such a name. The Church is the body of Christ, not the body of the Lord. The Lord's body in our chapter is that of which the bread was the emblem, as He Himself had said, "This is My body." Hence the man's guilt consisted in treating the Supper as an ordinary meal, not discerning in it that of which the elements were but figures. Now such conduct the Lord would not allow to go on unchecked. Self-judgment would indeed avert His judicial interference; but where that remained lacking, He Himself, the

Lord, would, and had interposed. Weakness, sickness, and death had visited many of the Corinthian assembly for these grave scandals; but perhaps, till pointed out by the apostle, they were scarcely aware of the reason for these divine visitations upon them. Yet there was grace in them. Because they were really Christians the Lord dealt thus with them, that they should not be condemned with the world.*

They had eaten unworthily. How many souls have been troubled about this, and have kept away from the table from not understanding the language and meaning of the apostle. No question was intended about their worthiness to be at the Supper. As Christians they were worthy; though of course, viewing the matter in another light, since grace alone gives one a place there, everyone must ever own himself unworthy of it. But the sin dealt with was the partaking of the Supper in an unworthy manner. Their ways at the table were what the apostle was writing of, and what the Lord had rebuked. They partook in an unworthy manner, not discerning the Lord's body. Such are guilty as respects His body and blood.

How then shall we provide against this? The Lord has told us, "Let a man examine himself, and so let him eat." What care does this evince that we should not render ourselves liable to judgment? What desire does it manifest on the Lord's part that all His people, unless disqualified by church-discipline, should come and eat?

---

* We may remark the terms employed in the passage. The saints are exhorted to examine or prove themselves ($\delta o \varkappa \iota \mu \acute{\alpha} \zeta \omega$) before they eat. If they judge or discern themselves ($\delta \iota \alpha \varkappa \rho \acute{\iota} \nu \omega$), they will not be judged ($\varkappa \rho \acute{\iota} \nu \omega$). When judged ($\varkappa \rho \acute{\iota} \nu \omega$), they are chastened or disciplined ($\pi \alpha \iota \delta \varepsilon \acute{\iota} \omega$), that they should not be condemned ($\varkappa \alpha \tau \alpha \varkappa \rho \acute{\iota} \nu \omega$) with the world.

CHAPTER XIV.

DISCIPLINE.

AS children of God we have to do with the Father o spirits, who trains us in His wisdom and grace This Hebrews xii. describes. As part of th Church of God we are subject to the chastening of th Lord, if, having done what is wrong, we fail to judge oui selves about it. Of this 1 Cor. xi. 30–32 treats. In ad dition to this, the Word teaches us how we should be have towards those who, reckoned amongst God's saints are not walking as becomes such; and how, under cei tain conditions specified in the New Testament, the disci pline of the house of God must be maintained, and exer cised by the assembly. Indifference to the walk o saints we should seek to be watchful against. Indiffer ence to the maintaining the purity of God's house we should zealously avoid. And while Heb. xii. and 1 Cor xi. show us how the Father, and the Lord, may deal with each of us as saints, other scriptures, to which we wil presently turn, teach us how we should deal individually with, and how the assembly should act towards, those whose walk and conversation call for notice and discoun tenance.

Very solemn, then, is the subject on which we are en tering. By it we are reminded of the holiness of the place—the house of God—of which all Christians form part. By it, too, we are constrained to remember what we all are by nature, who form part of God's habitation in the Spirit; and if called to act towards any walking wrongly, to express disapproval of their ways, it surely becomes us, when doing it, to remember that the same evil nature is in us which has been manifesting itself in them. A spirit of self-judgment—considering ourselves (Gal. vi. 1)—will befit us in such circumstances.

Now there are different ways of dealing with offending Christians. Under certain circumstances their brethren are, individually, to withdraw from them. Or, the assembly may have to take the matter up and rebuke them. Or, it may be called upon to resort to the severest measure, and put out the wicked person. Hence at the outset we can see that excommunication is not the only means of discipline sanctioned by the Word. In truth, it is the last step that can be resorted to, and indicates that nothing else can be done with the offender.

At Thessalonica an evil habit had already manifested itself, which the apostle called "walking disorderly"— brethren working not at all and seeking temporal support from others in the assembly. Against such a habit the apostle writes very strongly, charging the saints to discountenance it, charging those guilty of it to discontinue it: "We command you, brethren, in the name of our Lord Jesus Christ, that ye withdraw yourselves from every brother that walketh disorderly, and not after the tradition which they* received of us" (2 Thess. iii. 6). Such were his words to the saints. "Now them that are such (*i. e.* disorderly) we command and exhort in the Lord Jesus Christ, that with quietness they work and eat their own bread" (ver. 12). Such were his words to the offenders. Both parties were to see that the question was a serious one; and as they owned Jesus as Lord, they were to obey

---

*Some, as Lachmann and Tregelles, read, "Ye received." No uncial MS. supports the authorized version.

the injunctions given by His apostle. Eating the bread of others in idleness was no part of Christian teaching; nay, the contrary was enjoined. Exhortations to be liberal and brotherly to those really in need abound in the Word (Gal. vi. 6; Eph. iv. 28; 1 John iii. 17; 3 John 8); but eating the bread of others in idleness the Word distinctly forbids. To eat their own bread was to be the aim and desire of such as had been doing the contrary—learning of the apostle, who could labor night and day at his trade that he should not burden the saints. From all offenders after this sort Christians were to withdraw; and should there be one who did not obey the apostolic injunction communicated in writing, they were to note him, and not to keep company with him, that he might be ashamed (ver. 14).

Again, writing to the Romans (xvi. 17), he tells them to mark those that cause divisions and offences, or stumbling-blocks, contrary to the doctrine they had learned; and to avoid them. Divisions might arise amongst the saints—they were of the works of the flesh (Gal. v. 20)—but such as caused them were to be marked and turned from: the doctrine the saints had learned being the measure or standard by which they were to judge of and discern such. To avoid them is the apostolic injunction—the same word used by Peter when exhorting us to eschew evil (1 Pet. iii. 11). Now, in neither of these cases does the apostle Paul direct the saints to resort to the severe measure of excommunication. Withdrawing from them is not putting them out. Their place at the table they would still have, but the saints were to mark their disapproval of such ways by withdrawing in ordinary Christian intercourse from them, in the hope, as in the case of the disorderly walker, that such might be ashamed, and learning the evil of their course, forsake it.

Again, Titus is taught how to deal with a heretical man. First, he must admonish him; then, after a second admonition, if that failed, he was to reject or have done with him—(the same word as is used in 1 Timothy when enjoining him to turn from profane and old wives' fables iv. 7), and to decline the younger widows (ver. 11); for a heretical man does not of necessity mean one who denies the faith, but it is literally one who chooses his creed. Thus Paul, speaking of the Pharisees, to which party he had once belonged, called it the most straitest sect— αἱρεσις (*lit*, heresy)—of our religion (Acts. xxvi. 5). The sect of the Pharisees was regarded as orthodox in their creed; but Paul uses of them that word which has been ingrafted into our tongue, and with which most Englishmen are familiar, *heresy*. A heretical man, then, need not be one who denies any article of the Christian faith. He is a heretic who allows his mind or will to work in connection with doctrine, thereby producing or countenancing a sect; as we see from 1 Cor. xi. 19, where the apostle, writing of sects, uses the word *heresy*. Such a man was to be avoided, if admonition failed to have its due effect upon him. Patience in dealing with him there was to be; but if a second admonition failed to lead him to reject his error, he was to be avoided; for such an one "is subverted, and sinneth, being condemned of himself" (Titus iii. 11).

What care then there was to be on the part of all as to the walk and doctrine of each one! And how could it be otherwise, seeing that they were members of one body? Were they members of a denomination only, such questions might have been left to the leaders of the sect.

Had the tie been simply a congregational one, the members might have cast all responsibility on the rulers amongst them; but since they were members of one body, the ways of each one concerned all, and none could afford to be indifferent to such questions, nor to overlook such disorders and sins. Brotherly love too would be shown, not in keeping company with such, but in withdrawing from them; for true love seeks the welfare of its object.

Graver matters, however, might occur, where the tacit though marked disapproval of the saints, manifested by withdrawing from a brother or sister, would not meet the case. For such the Word also provides, and points out that, under certain conditions, the assembly itself must act, either in rebuking or excommunicating.

Rebuking, or convicting, we read of in 1 Tim. v. 20. This is called for in the case of such as sin, but where excommunication is not enjoined as the only way of dealing with the person. For there are cases where nothing but putting away from amongst Christians will be a sufficient dealing with the offender. There are other cases in which that extreme step is not enjoined. "Them that sin," writes the apostle, "rebuke [or convict; *i. e.* demonstrate their guilt] before all, that the rest may fear." "Them that sin." It does not say, "Them that have sinned," nor each time they have sinned. We all have sinned. We all do sin. But we are not all, each time we have failed, to be dealt with according to the directions here given to Timothy. A man might be overtaken in a fault as Galatians vi. 1 describes. Such a one was to be restored by the spiritual in a spirit of meekness, they considering themselves lest they also be tempted. Rebuking before all would, in such a case, be more than the Word warranted. Them that sin, we are told, are to be thus dealt with. Spiritual judgment may be needed to discern correctly about the case, and attention to the directions of Scripture will throw great light on the right treatment of cases as they come up. But where the assembly, judging the matter before God, sees that the individual who has failed comes under this category, rebuking before all is the injunction, that the rest may fear.

What a solemn duty this is which is cast upon the saints, that they who, if unwatchful, may themselves be liable to rebuke, are nevertheless to mark and give their distinct judgment and disapproval of a brother's ways as the Word directs, and that before all! The shame of a public conviction may tell upon the person; but the special object set before us in 1 Tim. v. 20 is the profit of all, "that the rest also may fear." With this before us, while carrying out the scriptural directions there will be no disposition to point the finger of scorn at the failing one, but to deepen in our hearts the sense of what we are by nature, and the need of true watchfulness, lest rebuke be righteously meted out to us.

But more severe measures still are set before us; for sin must not be trifled with, and the assembly has not only to deal with offenders, but to clear itself. Hence, if the offence calls for it, excommunication must take place; not simply because a brother has sinned—for who would then be at the table at all?—but because the person has sinned in such a way, that nothing short of it will meet the gravity of the case. What holy ground we are on! We are in the house of God; so we can make no compromise with evil, nor treat it with indifference.

When, then, must this severe step be taken? 1 Cor. v. 11 –13 gives clear indications: "I have written unto you not to keep company, if any man that is called a brother be a fornicator, or covetous, or an idolater, or a railer, or a drunkard, or an extortioner; with such a one no not to eat. For what have I to do to judge them also that are without? do not ye judge them that are within? But them that are without God judgeth. Put away* from yourselves that wicked person" (τὸν πονηρὸν). "A little leaven leaveneth the whole lump. Purge out the old leaven, that ye may be a new lump, as ye are unleavened. For even Christ our Passover is sacrificed: therefore let us keep the feast, not with old leaven, nor with the leaven of malice and wickedness; but with the unleavened bread of sincerity and truth" (vers. 6–8). A reference to Ex. xii. 15–19 will help us to understand the allusion. On the first day of the feast they were to put out all leaven from their houses, and throughout the feast no leaven was to be found there. The old leaven was to be put out at the commencement of the feast, and no fresh leaven was to be allowed within their doors while it lasted. Now this whole dispensation is to us the feast of unleavened bread; hence no leaven is to be allowed among us in God's house. If it comes in it must be put out.

Certain kinds of evil, then, if manifested, called for the excommunication of the offender. But should this course be restricted only to such as have sinned in the manner specified in 1 Cor. v. 11? Surely not. The last verse will help us in this matter: "Put out from among your-

---

*"Therefore," it is generally agreed, should be omitted; so also "for us" in ver. 7, and "therefore" in ver. 13. The omission of "therefore" in vers. 7, 13, makes the language more energetic.

selves the wicked person." Now a man might be a wicked person who had sinned in other ways than in the specific manner above described. For instance, if a teacher brought not the doctrine of Christ—not confessing Jesus Christ coming in flesh (not of course the mere fact, but the Person who is so characterized), such a one was not to be received amongst Christians. Even a woman was to shut her door against him, and not to bid him God-speed; *i.e.* hail or greet him with the ordinary friendly salutations; for any who did that would be a partaker of his evil deeds (2 John 7–11). Would such a one have a place at the Lord's table?

Again, if one brother had committed a trespass against another, and manifested a hardened spirit, which neither brotherly dealing nor the assembly's admonition could subdue, he was to be unto the one against whom he had sinned as a heathen man and a Publican (Matt. xviii. 17). Now a heathen man no Jew would admit to any ecclesiastical privileges (Acts xxi. 28, 29); with a Publican, or tax-gatherer, no Pharisee or scribe would associate. Hence the offender's position is clear, and what 1 Cor. v. 13 sets forth would be the only course open for the assembly. From how small a beginning such grave results might flow. The wicked person then would also be such a one as 2nd Epistle of John describes, and such a one too as Matt. xviii. 17 treats of; and at times it might help an assembly in deciding on a case if they asked themselves the question, "Has the one whose case is before us shown that he is a wicked person?" A Christian may have done wrong, and yet not be a wicked person. So also, if it be a question of rebuking, "Does the person whose case is in question come under the category of one who sins?"

Excommunication then, as the word implies, affects the person's rights, which as a Christian he has in common with others. By it he is put away from the company of the saints at the table till such time as he repents; and the assembly, judging that he has repented, restores him to his privileges in common with them. What then is to be the character of the carriage of the saints toward such a one? 1 Cor. v. 11 is explicit, and 2 John 10 agrees with it. It is not only that the offender cannot be received at the table, but those who have had social intercourse with him on Christian grounds must abstain from it. Are there not instances where, from ignorance of Scripture rules, and perhaps a mistaken desire to manifest brotherly love towards the guilty one, the discipline of the assembly, so far as it relates to ordinary friendly intercourse, has been entirely set aside, to the detriment of the offender, and to the loss really of all? The action of the assembly becomes thereby enfeebled, and a party feeling is in danger of being encouraged. If saints looked at the question in this light, "Can I have ordinary Christian friendly intercourse with one whose presence at His table my Lord refuses to sanction?" the right way of conducting ourselves towards such would be seen at a glance.

With what power then is the assembly invested? "Whatsoever ye shall bind on earth shall be bound in heaven: and whatsoever ye shall loose on earth shall be loosed in heaven" (Matt. xviii. 18). What care surely should be taken in the exercise of such discipline, lest we do on earth what heaven cannot ratify. How careful was Paul in the exercise of apostolic power. As careful, yet as firm, should the assembly be in the exercise of scriptural discipline.

CHAPTER XV.

ITS FUTURE.

IN Eph. v. 27 we learn the purpose of Christ respecting the Church. He will present to Himself that pearl of great price (Matt. xiii. 46), the Church glorious, not having spot or wrinkle, or any such thing. In that same epistle we are informed of the Church's everlasting continuance (iii. 21). From Heb. xii. 23 we have been taught how distinct will be its position in heaven from that of the Old Testament saints, there termed "the spirits of just men made perfect." In Rev. xix. 7, 8 we read of the marriage of the Lamb, and of His wife having made herself ready. Her bridal attire is there also stated to be fine linen, white and clean, which is the righteous deeds ($\tau \grave{\alpha}\ \delta\iota\varkappa\alpha\acute{\omega}\mu\alpha\tau\alpha$) of the saints.

So far, then, we read of the Bride as fully answering to the desires of Christ, with whom she will be for ever and ever. But in none of these scriptures to which we have turned is she described as visible to the eyes of people on earth; yet she will be seen by them. And John, who in vision beheld her as the world will see her, has described her appearance and special characteristics (Rev. xxi. 9–xxii. 5) when she was shown to him by an angel. It was one of the seven angels, who had the seven last plagues, who took him in the spirit into the wilderness to see the great whore (Rev. xvii.). It was one of the same angelic company which carried him in the spirit to a great and high mountain, and showed him the holy* city Jerusalem, descending out of heaven from God in her millennial character and glory, when for the first time the whole Assembly, composed only of those who are members of His body, will be displayed to a wondering universe. But that cannot take place till the Lamb appears in His millennial glory. The woman, the whore, Babylon, is content to reign without Him. The Bride is satisfied to wait for Him. Then the parody of Satan, revealed in the Apocalypse, and so known to God's saints, will be apparent to all. The true bride is a city, a metropolis—the metropolis of the universe. The great whore is a city, which in John's day was reigning over the kings of the earth, the metropolis of the then so-called habitable earth (Luke ii. 1). With gold, and precious stones, and pearls, is the woman of Rev. xvii. described as bedecked. Gold, and precious stones, and pearls, will be seen to form part of the splendor of the heavenly city. To Babylon flowed the commerce and wealth of the world (xviii.). Unto the heavenly city (not into it) will the glory and honor of the nations flow, and to it will the kings of the earth bring their glory. So far is the parallel; now for the contrast.

The whore is decked in all her meretricious splendor to captivate the kings of the earth. The Bride, when prepared to meet the Lamb, is arrayed in fine linen, clean and white. Not that she puts on ornaments for *Him;* but when she is to be publicly displayed as the Lamb's wife, gold, precious stones and pearls are marked feat-

---

* The four uncial MSS. which have preserved this part of the book agree in omitting the word "*great.*" "Great" is an epithet applied to the whore (xvii. 1; xix. 2); "holy" is the characteristic term used of the Bride (xxi. 2, 10).

ures in her appearance (xxi. 18–21). It was in the wilderness, and seated on the beast, that John saw the whore. It is as descending from heaven, and having the glory of God, that he beheld the Bride. And further, there was seen in the holy Jerusalem that which Satan could not imitate—the presence of God, and the throne of God. No temple (ναὸς) was there; for the Lord God Almighty was the temple thereof, and the Lamb. No need had the city of the light of the sun, nor of the moon; for the glory of God enlightened it, and the Lamb was the lamp (λύχνος) thereof. There also was the throne of God and of the Lamb; and in undimmed and unceasing brightness shall the Lord God shine upon His servants, who shall reign for ever and ever (xxi. 22, 23; xxii. 3–5).

The Bride, then, as John here sees her, has been already presented to the Bridegroom (xix. 7). The holy temple, so long in building, has now been completed; and God, who by the Holy Ghost now inhabits His dwelling-place on earth, is here seen at length enshrined in His temple. The desires of Christ about His Church have been fulfilled; the plans of God about His temple have been completed; and those on earth can see what the Church is to Christ and to God. It is a holy city indeed, into which nothing that defileth can enter. It is a select place, too, into which none have the right of entry but such as are written in the Lamb's book of life (xxi. 27).

Here, then, those two lines of truth which run throughout the New Testament (Kingdom truth and Church truth) at last converge. The Lamb's wife is the metropolis of the universe. Both characters are hers. The one is not merged into the other. She does not cease to be the

Lamb's wife because she is displayed as the holy city Jerusalem. Presented, then, in this double character, the nations on earth during millennial times will have to own her. As the Bride now, the wife then, of course she stands in a peculiar and special relation to the Lamb. As the seat of God's throne, and enlightened by His glory, the glory and honor of the nations will be brought unto her. Light, too, and healing will proceed from her —light in which the nations* will walk; healing from the leaves of the tree of life in her midst, of which they will stand in need. The world may not care for the saints of God now; men will find that they cannot do without the Church of God then.

On earth will be seen the city of the Lord, the Zion of the Holy One of Israel, unto which the world's wealth will flow, and which the kingdoms and nations upon earth must likewise serve. Within her walls will be found God's earthly house, the house of prayer for all people (Isa. lvi. 7); and year by year must those left of the nations which came against Jerusalem repair thither to worship the King, the Lord of hosts, and to keep the Feast of Tabernacles (Zech. xiv. 16). Features, too, corresponding to those of the heavenly city will be seen, as Ezek. xlvii. tells us, in the earthly one. Waters imparting life will proceed from her midst, corresponding to the river of the water of life in the city on high. And all trees for meat will grow on the banks of that stream, their fruit for meat, their leaves for medicine. But the tree of life will be on high, and the light of the earthly city will be derived from that which shines down through the holy Jerusalem (Isa. lx. 19, 20); and God's tabernacle will in

---

* We should omit, with all uncial MSS., "of them which are saved."

the fullest way be over His people Israel then* (Ezek. xxxvii. 27); for the heavenly city will be above and over the earthly one. The holy Jerusalem is the Lamb's wife. To the earthly one Jehovah will show Himself as her husband (Isa. liv. 5).

Such is the divine arrangement for millennial times. The kingdom of God will be established in power; but that cannot take place apart from the display of the Lamb's wife as the holy city Jerusalem on high. Then all will see how fully indeed is the revelation of the Church the filling up of the word of God; for without it, apart from it, God's purposes in connection with the Kingdom cannot be completed.

With the description of the last attempt to subvert God's order upon earth by the hosts of Gog encompassing the camp of the saints and the beloved city (Rev. xx. 9), the history of Zion ends. Not so that of the holy Jerusalem. Heaven and earth will pass away, but the the Church will abide. And when out of the melted elements and burnt earth God will make new heavens and a new earth, in both which ($\grave{\epsilon}\nu$ $o\hat{\iota}s$) will dwell righteousness, the holy city, new Jerusalem, will come down out of heaven from God a second time. Time will have made no change in her appearance; for John saw her, in the eternal state, prepared as a bride adorned for her husband. And then in a new character will she have to do with earth and with men; for a voice out of heaven (or, as the two oldest uncial MSS. read, "the throne") was heard, saying, "Behold, the tabernacle of God is with men, and He will tabernacle with them" (chap. xxi. 3). During the Millennium He who sits upon the throne will tabernacle over His saints (chap. vii. 15). In the eternal

---

* *Over* them, not *with* them, seems the thought in Ezekiel.

state He will tabernacle with men, and grief, and sin, and death, will exist no more upon earth. The whore will long have passed away from earth (chap. xvii. 16). The earthly Jerusalem, as far as we know, will also be found no longer; but the new Jerusalem will abide for ever and ever.

Here ends the revelation about the Church or Assembly of God, telling us that she will never cease to exist in her distinctive character and relation both to the Lord Jesus Christ and to God. She comes forth in the eternal state prepared as a bride adorned for her husband. She is seen in the eternal state as the tabernacle of God. The object of Christ's love in the past, in the present, and in the future; a subject of divine revelation, and forming an integral part of the counsels of God, precious to Christ and to Him; such is the Church, the body and the Bride of Christ; the house, the habitation, the holy temple, and the tabernacle of God.

www.ingramcontent.com/pod-product-compliance
Lightning Source LLC
Chambersburg PA
CBHW071434160426
43195CB00013B/1893